Objects in Context:
Theorizing Material Culture

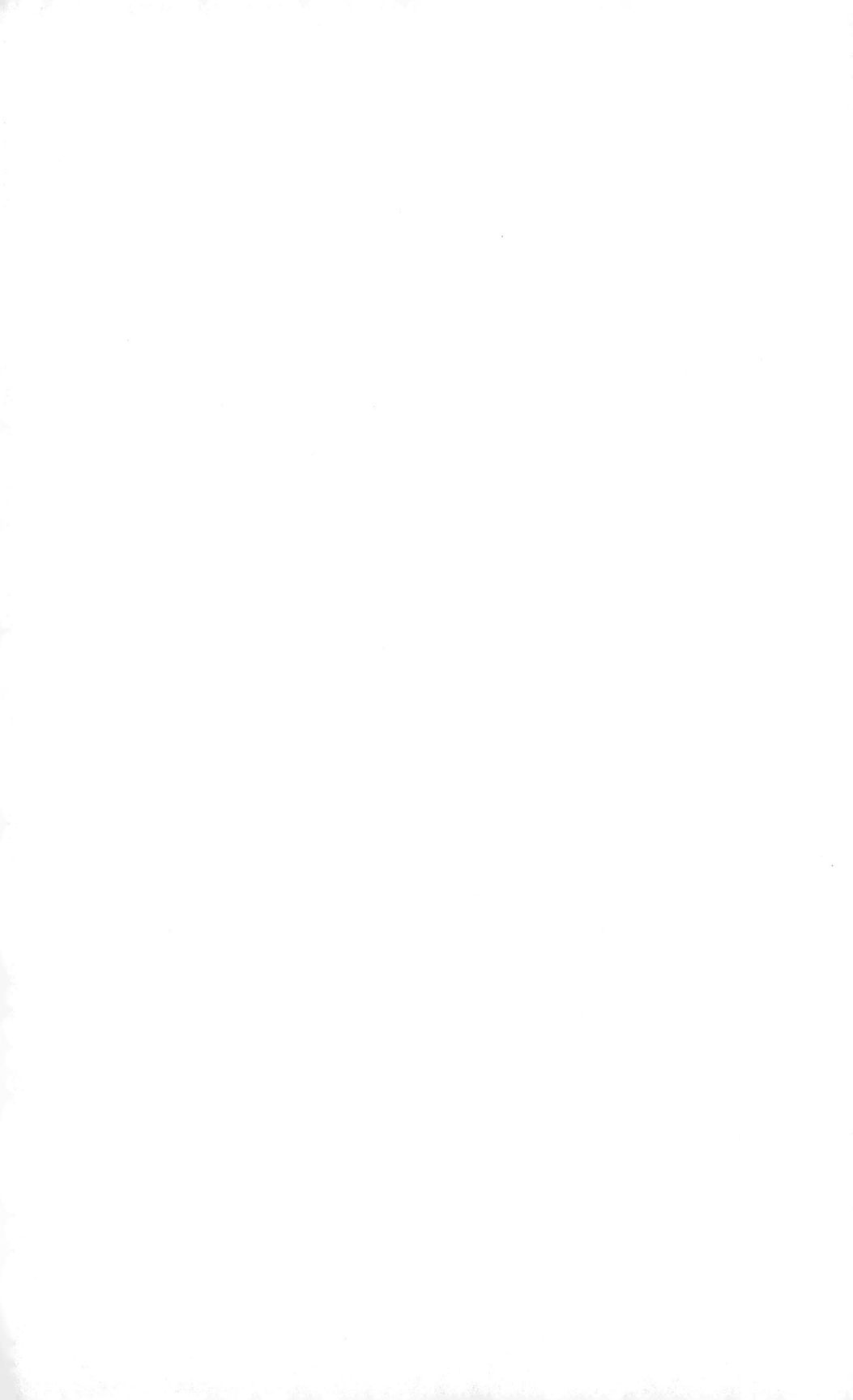

Objects in Context
Theorizing Material Culture

Stephanie Anderson & Cierra Webster
Co-Editors

Objects in Context: Theorizing Material Culture

© Stephanie Anderson and Cierra Webster 2013
Printed in Canada

ISBN: 978-1-304-36427-2

Layout design by M. Curtis Allen and Cierra Webster
Cover design by M. Curtis Allen

Contents

Acknowledgements

This book would not have been possible without the hard work, enthusiasm, advice, and support of many generous individuals to whom we owe an incredible debt of gratitude. Firstly we would like to thank the Department of Visual Arts at Western University for providing a supportive and encouraging environment within which creative and ambitious projects such as the one at hand are able to take seed and thrive. Our sincere thanks go especially to Dr. Joy James, whose active excitement for the project has greatly contributed to its success, and to Joanne Gribbon, for her unwavering enthusiasm and the countless tasks she undertook to ensure the smooth coordination of various components of this undertaking.

For their generous financial support, we thank the Department of Visual Arts, the Faculty of Arts and Humanities, the Faculty of Social Sciences, the Centre for the Study of Theory and Criticism, and the Departments of Philosophy, Women's Studies and Feminist Research, Modern Languages and Literatures, and Film Studies. We also thank the McIntosh Gallery and its staff, which provided the venue and catering for the opening reception of the conference from which the papers herein derive. And we would like to especially thank James Patten, Director of the McIntosh Gallery, for unreservedly welcoming our proposal to extend the conference events into the gallery space, and for his genuine engagement, guidance, and support in the subsequent weeks of planning and executing what turned out to be an incredibly positive and fruitful event.

Furthermore, we offer special thanks to two individuals who have been invaluable to the launch of this publication. To Samantha E. Angove, who was integral to the initial conception and vision of the project and whose time and energy has continued to be a driving force through its mutation into this alternative format. And to M. Curtis Allen, who generously took up the time-consuming task of cover design and layout, and for whom we cannot overstate our appreciation.

Finally, of course, we would like to thank all of the contributors to this volume for their initial interest and continued investment in bringing the publication to fruition, for enduring several laborious rounds of edits, and of course for their engaging and thought-provoking essays. We are excited to have brought together such an interesting range of perspectives and insights from a group of truly wonderful scholars.

About the Contributors

Stephanie Anderson is a PhD candidate in Art and Visual Culture at Western University. Her MA thesis, titled *'Use it or Lose it': Inuit Art and the 'Soft Power' of Canadian Cultural Diplomacy*, explores the historical representation of Inuit art and culture in the Canadian 'national image' in relation to the shifting terrains of Canadian cultural policy, diplomatic relations, and indigenous politics since WWII, and more generally in relation to the widespread reconceptualization of 'culture' as an economic expedient in the current era of neoliberal globalization. Her current research explores intersections between contemporary craft practices, the creative economy, labour, and materiality in post-industrial societies. Related areas of interest include somaesthetics, tactile epistemology, worldbuilding, and the politics of utopia and nostalgia in the twenty-first century.

Samantha E. Angove holds a Master of Arts degree in Art History from Western University. Her thesis, *We Come in Piece,* is a timely critique of the rise of postcolonial science fiction exhibitions within the contemporary art world. Samantha has won several awards and scholarships – but has yet to receive that *elusive* SSHRC. Her guilty pleasures are contemporary indigenous art, architecture design, and French romcoms. In 2012, she co-curated the 'Negotiation within the Frame' exhibitions at the McIntosh Gallery in London, Ontario. Samantha is currently enjoying her first 'gap year,' selling art on a cruise ship.

Rachel Fagiano received her undergraduate degree from Bard College with a Bachelor of Arts in Political Science. This past January, Fagiano completed her Master of Arts in Caribbean and Latin American Studies with an Advanced Certificate in Museum Studies at New York University. She currently works at the Tinker Foundation Inc. focusing on the U.S./Latin American relations portfolio for the foundation. Fagiano also works freelance for various arts institutions, including galleries and museums, developing educational materials focused on identity building. In the past, she has worked and volunteered for numerous organizations with a focus on Latin America and the Arts including: Central American Legal Assistance, El Museo del Barrio, and the Americas Society. The majority of her work centers on issues of race and racisms in the Americas.

Hannah Jocelyn has a Bachelor of Arts in Honours English Literature from Concordia University and a Master of Arts in Humanities from York University. She currently lives in Brooklyn and attends New York University for a Master of Arts in Humanities and Social Thought at the Draper School. Her subject of inquiry is how the cultural, social, political, and economic relationship between Canada and the United States can be read in contemporary writing by women.

Andrew Kingston is a Master of Arts student at the Centre for the Study of Theory and Criticism at Western University. He holds a Bachelor of Arts in philosophy, and is currently writing his thesis on Hegel's *Philosophy of Nature*, putting it into conversation with twentieth-century literary theory. Among his academic interests are the ideas of negativity, nonsense, general economy, and materiality.

Emma Kreiner is a writer and photographer interested in the ways in which film and photography represent and affect people in urban spaces. She is a Master of Arts candidate in the Art History program at Concordia University in Montreal, has a Bachelor of Arts in History and Art History from Queen's University (Canada), and spent a semester studying film and media theory at University College Maastricht (The Netherlands). Under the supervision of Dr. Martha Langford, her thesis explores the filmic documentation of the Montreal neighbourhood of Saint-Henri.

Taien Ng-Chan is a writer, media artist, and SSHRC-funded scholar in the PhD in Humanities at Concordia University. Her areas of investigation focus on the poetics of everyday urban life through experimental cinema and cartography. She has published one book/CD and two anthologies, and written drama for stage, screen, and radio. Her most recent work, *Detours: Poetics of the City*, involved collaboration to produce site-specific digital works for interactive artist maps of Montreal, including videos to watch while riding public transit. Her website is www.soyfish.net.

Samantha Oswald is currently completing her Master of Architecture degree at the University of Waterloo, where her field of study is brick in all its forms. Her research has taken her from Rome, Italy, to Warsaw, Poland, and most recently to the countryside outside London, England, where she has experimented with custom brick-making. Her profound belief is that a greater understanding of the power of material in architecture will lead to more efficient and meaningful environments.

Kaitlynn McQueston was born in Toronto, Ontario. She recently completed her Bachelor of Fine Arts at York University in 2012. McQueston was also nominated for the international sculpture competition and the BMO First Art Competition in both sculpture and painting. She has showcased her work in Montreal, Toronto, and Victoria. Presently, she is an Master of Fine Arts candidate at the University of Victoria in Visual Arts. Starting in fall of 2013, McQueston will be working as a researcher in the Digital Humanities Maker Lab at the University of Victoria.

Boké Saisi is a Master of Arts student at York University in the Joint Communication and Culture program specializing in Media and Culture and Politics and Policy. She received a Bachelor of Journalism from Ryerson University with a minor in Sociology. Her research interests include: critical race studies, race, class, and gender representation, social inequality and social justice, political economy, and international relations in news media. Her current Master's thesis examines the Africanization of poverty within North American news media, interrogating the ways in which transcontinental blackness and poverty are concurrently constructed within the medium.

Angela Silver is a Montreal-based artist examining notions of absence through the residue of language. Using artifacts from writing systems she seeks to restructure and reorder language systems. Drawing on performance, she re-tools obsolete writing objects as a strategy to reconsider speech, writing and communication itself. Her work has been exhibited and performed at DAC in Brooklyn, DARE-DARE in Montreal, Quebec City, Beverly, Toronto, Rome, Calgary, Pittsburgh, and the Netherlands. Coinciding with her independent practice, she has a collaborative practice with Andrew King. Silvers' practice and research have been generously supported by, a J.W. McConnell Fellowship and a Social Sciences Humanities Research Council Fellowship. She is the director of the Institute for pure and applied poetics. She is a PhD candidate in Cultural Studies at Queen's University in Kingston. Her work can be seen at angelasilver.com.

Corinne Thiessen Hepher is a Master of Fine Arts candidate in the graduate program at the University of Lethbridge. Her current art practice includes sculpture, drawing, video, and performance along with an investigation into transgressive bodies and deviant behaviour. She uses the playful imagery of the grotesque to comment on gender, politics, social structures, and interpersonal relationships.

Cierra Webster holds a Master of Arts degree from the Department of Visual Arts at Western University. Her MA thesis examined homonationalism through three different contemporary art practices, bringing together postcolonial, queer, and canonical critiques. At Western, she furthermore taught Art Theory and provided guest lectures on 'Early 20th Century Art' and 'Art & Advertising.' Cierra has also presented at conferences internationally on topics ranging from activism and subversive politics, to contemporary queer theory and institutional critique. In addition, Cierra enjoys baking and everything related to Harry Potter.

Introduction

Stephanie Anderson
Samantha Angove
Cierra Webster

Introduction

Stephanie Anderson, Samantha Angove, and Cierra Webster

> *"I forgot one," Samantha mumbled. She turned to Cierra and asked her to watch what she was about to do. Ttzzzp— similar to the dreadful act of ripping off a bandage, Samantha tore the (Re)Activating Objects poster off of the Visual Art's bulletin board.*

There was something memorable in the moments following that unassuming gesture. As we slowly proceeded to the elevators with our hands full, we quietly reflected on the weekend's success and the ambivalence we felt with its resolve. It was clear that the bottles of champagne we held in our hands would be enjoyed at another time — during an occasion that was not marked with exhaustion. We both headed home happy and satisfied, but also with tired smiles on our faces.

While writing this introduction to the *Objects in Context* publication, that feeling we got in the elevators came back. It is a feeling of discomfort and quieted exhilaration that happens while reflecting on the success of your own event and, hopefully, its continuing lifespan.

Objects in Context: Theorizing Material Culture came together out of a graduate student conference that took place at Western University (London, Ontario, Canada) in March of 2013. The conference, entitled *(Re)Activating Objects: Social Theory and Material Culture* brought together over 100 delegates from across Canada and the United States to investigate the ways that material culture provides a lens to examine the structures of our socio-cultural-economic worlds. As such, participants from a variety of disciplines presented papers addressing a wide range of fundamental and theoretical questions about social constructions, social politics, and social ethics. We asked candidates to 'activate' objects that are under-theorized and/or 'reactivate' objects with shifting or multiple ideologies. Ultimately, we asked, what can objects tell us about the worlds in which we live?

The story of this conference began on an average day in August 2012 as two graduate students sat down to talk about the potential of organizing an international graduate-student conference. We had big plans. As co-organizer Samantha Angove explained in an interview with *FUSE Magazine*, "co-organizer Cierra Webster and I have pretty similar worldviews and so when Cierra came to me and asked, or *told*, me that we should organize a graduate student conference for the Visual Arts department, it almost went without saying that it was going to be situated within critical questions about the social world" (Borland 2013). In these beginning stages, we wanted to make the conference theme general enough so that (almost) everyone could see their research within the topic. And because of this, we certainly risked organizing a conference that lacked cohesion. However, the result was far better than we could have imagined. Due to this broader theme, we received over 180 conference abstract submissions from all across Canada, the United States, and Europe.

When the conference weekend finally began, *(Re)Activating Objects* opened with a keynote talk by Dr. Lane Relyea. Lane Relyea is a cultural observer, critic, curator, theorist, author, and educator. He is also the chair of Art Theory & Practice from Northwestern University and editor of *Art Journal*. At the conference, Relyea's keynote talk, entitled 'Overdoing it Ourselves: The Belabored Object Between Social and Short-Term Contract,' examined the effects of communication networks on artistic practice and its context(s). The talk was followed by a very lively and fruitful discussion period and reception at the McIntosh Gallery located on Western University's campus.

Following the very successful opening night, *(Re)Activating Objects* hosted sixty presenters from twenty-eight different universities over the course of two days. The committee selected papers that address the ways that material culture can facilitate critical analyses of conventional historical narratives, but that also, through analysis of their object, imagine or propose future directions. As such, the presenters discussed material culture in ways that extend well beyond an object's utilitarian purposes. Our definition of object or material culture was also quite open, so-to-speak. Delegates presented papers about objects ranging from passports and pennies, to custom-made scrap metal guitars, gravestones, embroidery, candy, bumper stickers, paperclips, Hollywood film, the body, and a number of art objects and projects, to mention just a few.

In the aftermath of the conference, it is our hope that this publication will serve as a way to extend the timely and dynamic dialogue that took place over this productive and exciting weekend. As such, the selection of papers that follow address several main themes that emerged from the dizzying diversity of topics that characterized *(Re)Activating Objects*, grouped by unifying threads of inquiry and analysis. The essays that compose the first section are broadly interested in issues of space, architecture, and the built environment, addressing issues around the social understanding of place and of the bodies that inhabit such spaces. The second section brings together essays that, in different yet mutually informative ways, interrogate objects relating to nation(s), nationhood, and economy. Finally, the third section addresses issues of race and racisms, highlighting the ways in which a focus on material objects can contribute to, complicate, and nuance our understanding of contemporary and historical racial tensions. Interspersed with these theoretical and art historical papers, we have also chosen to highlight the work of emerging and established artists who interrogate these themes through their own material practices.

Opening the first section is 'Fired Ground: Warsaw's History in Brick' by Samantha Oswald. In this chapter, the role of brick in Warsaw, Poland is taken as a case study to demonstrate the profound influence of materiality in the built environment. In today's image-centric culture, the identity of a city is often inferred solely through observations of its skyline. At ground level, hidden beneath layers of plaster or tucked as ruins between larger buildings, a different story begins to emerge, one in which the humble brick, the base unit of construction for much of Warsaw's history, takes on the role of protagonist. Telling Warsaw's story through Oswald's examination of brick allows the full complexity of its multiple historical narratives to emerge, since at different points in time, brick has come to stand for contradicting concepts: freedom and oppression, solidity and ruin, humanization and monotony, and legislation and self-organization. The author's personal experience grounds this investigation in the material reality of the Polish capital; brick becomes a means of understanding both the cultural context of a city and architecture's power to shape it.

The second chapter continues an analysis of the built environment through the lens of two films that depict the Montreal, Quebec neighbourhood of Saint-Henri. Written by Emma Kreiner, 'Saint-Henri and the Urban Uncanny' analyses the ways in which the district's architecture was depicted in Hubert Aquin's *À Saint-Henri le cinq septembre* (1962) and Shannon Walsh's *À Saint-Henri, le 26 août* (2011), and how various urban organization and edifice conducts and transmits social meanings. In particular, this chapter interrogates the representation of Saint-Henri's post-industrial landscape, and the ways in which both its stagnant nature and its subsequent filmic portrayal affected the residents of the neighbourhood, described by Aquin as 'dying.' In a telling contrast, Kreiner also outlines the more recent gentrification of Saint-Henri, wherein new housing developments have allotted agency to a bourgeois population, while the original working class inhabitants have been disempowered by increasing rents and their ensuing displacement. A close reading of these two filmic depictions reveals social and political implications of representing urban squalor, architectural decay, as well as the more recent gentrification that has contributed to the condition of groundlessness and ambiguity in Saint-Henri.

Our next section begins with Andrew Kingston's 'Ghosts of the Economic Image: Blanchot, Bataille, and the Non-circulation of the Canadian Penny.' Kingston takes as his object of inquiry the Canadian penny and its discontinuation by the Canadian government in 2013. Though this might seem to be of little consequence, the author questions what the elimination of such a simple economic unit can tell us about economy in general— its limits, its potentialities. Drawing on the work of Maurice Blanchot, Georges Bataille, and Surrealism, Kingston explores the significance of this change in coinage. The penny literally constitutes the base and possibility of economic transaction. To remove the penny as the basis of exchange, is not only a structural reconfiguration of economics, but also quite clearly reveals its arbitrary, and in Bataille's phrasing, 'restricted' character. The removal from circulation of the penny thereby symbolically subverts the abstract social function of capital, while at the same time giving a real impetus toward the imaginary, toward an imagination that exceeds the overly dominant, yet narrowly determined bounds of global capitalism. In short, Kingston proposes that the ultimate evacuation of meaning of the penny enacts a rematerialization of the aesthetic, raising it from the entombment of an economic symbolism. Yet precisely because the penny is at present an economic object, in its elimination it simultaneously can perform a critique of the restricted economy from which it originated.

In this same section, Hannah Jocelyn continues with an examination of national objects. In her chapter, 'The Passport and the Holder,' Jocelyn begins with the observation that in this evermore 'globalized' and regulated world, owning a passport is seemingly ubiquitous. Whether a person is an international traveler or not, the passport has become as necessary as a birth certificate. For those without a passport, the world is a very different – limited – place. However, she argues that this object is not merely a claim to nationality, a record of journey, or a permit home. Instead, the passport is a socially-constructed device. Without our having collectively agreed to its meaning, the passport would be nothing more than an unflattering picture. Moreover, the passport is an indicator of status, of belonging. This chapter is particularly concerned with what a passport signifies. Within its pages, the passport holds issues of identity, exclusion, marginalization, class, nationalism, transnationality, globalization, and more. The author asks, what does having a passport do for the holder? *To* the holder? Where do non-holders stand? What does the importance of the passport illustrate about the current framework of the world?

In the final section of *Objects in Context*, Boké Saisi begins with her chapter entitled 'The Hijab and the Hoodie: Dress as Politics and Politicized Dress.' In March of 2012, Trayvon Martin, a seventeen-year-old African American boy was shot to death by a neighbourhood watchman in his gated community in Southern Florida. Martin, clad with Skittles and an iced tea, was wearing a dark, hooded sweatshirt at the time of his death. In the aftermath of the shooting, the 'hoodie' — a seemingly mundane sporting good often associated with concealment and criminality — was used to protest the death that was viewed as a cogent example of racial tension and racial profiling in the United States. Similarly, the hijab has been viewed with Orientalist meanings, in that veiling is perceived as a symbol of Muslim misogyny and an impending Islamist threat. However, the hijab is also an active article of political protest. In this chapter, Saisi compares the image and materiality of the hoodie and the hijab, arguing that in the aftermath of the Trayvon Martin shooting, the hoodie, like the hijab, was used as a symbol of political contestation by its wearers, thus resisting views of the material object as a marker of criminality and fear. In this way, the author highlights that the hijab and the hoodie, as materials in themselves, do not represent criminality, fear, protest, or resistance. It is the meanings imbued on the materials that render them suspect or subversive. As Saisi argues, ultimately both material items, the hijab and the hoodie, enable the wearers an agency of protest.

The last chapter of the publication also seeks to understand racial tensions in the United States. '(Re)Activating History: Race, Violence, Materiality and Interactive Technologies in the Museum' by Rachel Fagiano suggests new modes of displaying sensitive materials in museum spaces. Using the Allen-Littlefield collection of lynching photographs on postcards, eventually exhibited under the title *Without Sanctuary: Lynching Photography in America*, as a case study, Fagiano highlights some of the fundamental polemic issues present in museum practice in the United States. Currently, the discourse surrounding the display of lynching images within museums has become mired along an axis of public good vs. public harm. The author notes that opponents of the public display of these images argue that the exhibitions recreate the atmosphere of spectacle under which lynchings originally occurred while simultaneously numbing the general public to violent race-based imagery. Proponents of the public exhibition of lynching images argue that these displays help to inform the American public of the country's racist past and prevent future race-based crime. It is within this debate that Fagiano specifically argues that the lynching images within the Allen-Littlefield collection demand a reframing that focuses on the materiality of the images by positioning them as photographic postcards rather than as purely photographic documentation. In doing so, individuals involved in future displays of these images can help to understand the role that these past events play in shaping the racial attitudes of today.

As noted, we have chosen to highlight four practicing artists in 'Artist Profile' sections dispersed throughout the publication. Taien Ng-Chan, Kaitlynn McQueston, Corinne Thiessen Hepher, and Angela Silver use their material practices to engage with a range of practical, political, and theoretical issues and concerns and thus initiate an extended dialogue which complements and nuances the essays described above. The artists included in this publication offer to the reader a succinct snapshot of the theoretical interests and engagements of emerging artists today.

Taien Ng-Chan is based in Montreal, Quebec where she is completing a PhD at Concordia University. In her contribution to *Objects in Context*, Ng-Chan explores the symbolic power of the L'Acadie Fence, a chain-link fence that stands on the border of two very different neighbourhoods in Montreal. Ng-Chan shows that, in photographing the entire fence during different times and seasons, the focusing, framing, editing, and compositing of her work have all become tools to explore the materiality of the fence itself. The final digital photo work consists of an extremely long collage with insets showing specific details such as a patched-up hole (a challenge to the boundary) and the signs on the gates as well as the places for locks. Theoretically, Ng-Chan's project looks at the L'Acadie Fence through a Thirdspace analysis, as proposed by geographer Edward Soja. After his trialectical theories, Ng-Chan offers a Firstspace (spatial) analysis through a photographic collage work of the L'Acadie Fence. Her Secondspace (historical) analysis traces the development of the two neighbourhoods, one as a designed and planned suburban city by Canada's first landscape architect, the other as an 'unplanned' working-class immigrant enclave. Finally, the Thirdspace (social) analysis gives a personal, subjective account of the lived spaces that make up the artist's neighbourhoods, as she passes through the fence almost every day. Ng-Chan's work elucidates that thirdspace is a critical space that keeps in mind the specific power relations that have contributed to the development of these neighbourhoods.

Currently based in Victoria, British Columbia, Kaitlynn McQueston's art works aim to expose the nuances of Canadian labour politics and the industrial material world. Using needle felting techniques, McQueston created a fabric V8 engine including all working parts called 'The Felt Machine.' Alongside this piece, she produced videos of wood grain texture slowly appearing on her skin. Entitled 'Pornaganda,' the artist plays with the reversal of traditional advertising methods that employ sexual seduction as subtle or hidden weapons of persuasion. In this way, McQueston's body imprints and fabric machines both interrogate the complementary processes of labour politics and sensual perception. She uses this juxtaposition to understand cultural tensions between the industrial world and our desires.

Corinne Thiessen Hepher is a Master of Fine Arts candidate at the University of Lethbridge. The next artist profiled in the *Objects in Context* publication, she interrogates 'gendered' objects. Thiessen Hepher particularly collects ephemera such as birth control pill packaging, pregnancy tests, and instructions for feminine hygiene products. In this way, she acts as an imposter-archaeologist by reassembling objects to create new narratives and new meaning to playfully reexamination conceptions of empirical knowledge. She shows that gleaning marginalized objects is an act of privileging the other, while exploring the taxonomy of culture. In her art practice, Thiessen Hepher combines objects, found or transformed, and creates body extensions and mechanical, motorized sculptures. She also places her body in the work and performs socially-constructed 'deviant' gestures such as hysteria that have a significant gendered history. Therefore, in her contribution to this publication, the artist revels in taboo subjects to expose historical and contemporary power discrepancies.

Angela Silver is the final artist spotlighted in this publication. Montreal-based and presently attending Queen's University (Kingston, Ontario), Silver investigates obsolete writing technologies motivated not from any sense of nostalgia but to reorder the artefacts and paraphernalia associated with outdated machines and their processes. In her performances, the artist explores the gap between traditional processes of communication and corporeal experiences. In this work, Silver questions the authority of text by operating *within* this gap: between conventional language structures and experience. She also deconstructs and recontextualizes systems of communication by repurposing writing machines and their paraphernalia. By forming radical ways the body can perform communication, Silver seeks to examine the representation of language, simultaneously looking at western society's complicated, and oftentimes oversimplified, relationship with information and communication.

The diverse range of topics addressed within these pages are united by a shared interest in how material objects can enhance our understanding of various socio-political and economic processes, systems, structures, and identities. Together, they will open up a critical space in which to interrogate and expand dominant modes of research and analysis. Enjoy!

Taien Ng-Chan

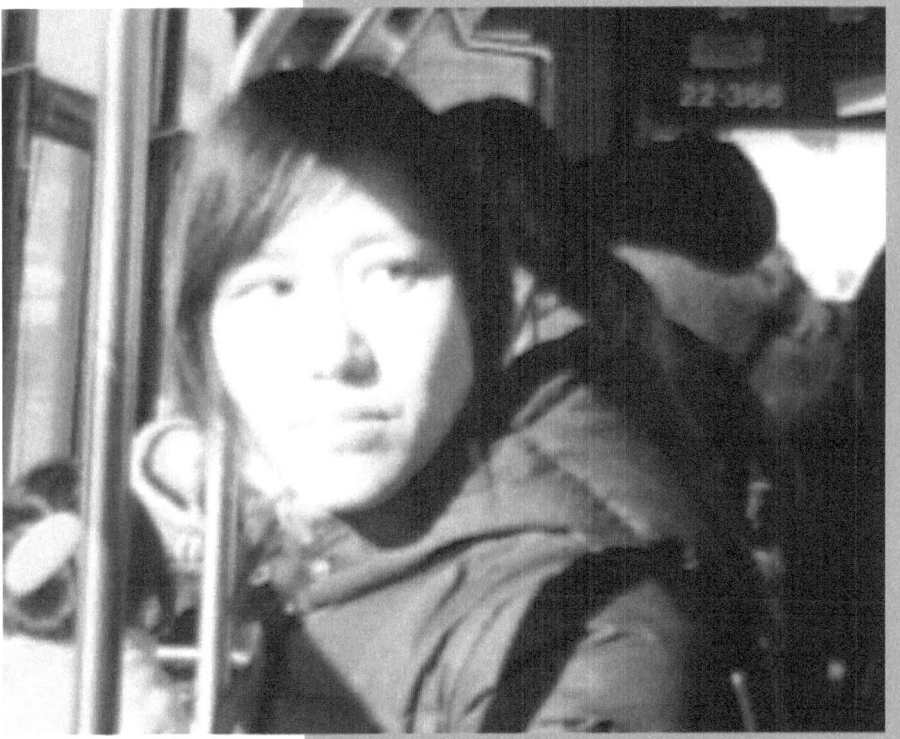

L'Acadie Fence: A Series of Views

Taien Ng-Chan

Fences

There are many views of a fence.

John Brinkerhoff Jackson, known as the founder of cultural landscape studies in North America, thought highly of fences, stating "a boundary is what binds us all together in a group, that which excludes the outsider or stranger. The boundary creates neighbours; it is the symbol of law and order and permanence" (Jackson 1980, 115). A fence allows us to balance the private and the public to the degree that each of us is comfortable. A good backyard fence is essential if one values privacy in a densely populated neighbourhood. And in the summertime, fences extend small living spaces to the outdoors, making the private more public as the neighbours move out into their backyards. High wooden fences, or wire fences with plastic weavings, imply that the owners do not want to see their neighbours; open wire fences invite interaction. I know most well those neighbours whose fences I can see through. When I stroll down the alleys, I see them gardening or barbequing. Often we greet each other or nod.

Lucy Maynard Salmon took the opposite view to Jackson's. Salmon was a historian who began writing in the late 1800s, one of the earliest researchers to take on the local as an important site of analysis. She argued that fences mean "isolation, separation, and lack of common interest; the absence of the fence means community life, mutual aid, toleration, and joint pleasures and opportunities" (Salmon 2001, 79). Clearly, the whys and wherefores of fences greatly influence whether they are useful or detrimental. The majority of fences in this city are relatively benign, and indeed, simply practical.

One particular fence in Montreal does not, however, seem benign: the Acadie Boulevard Fence that runs between Jean-Talon Boulevard to the south and the #40 highway to the north. I cross this fence almost daily in my walk from Parc-Extension (Parc-X), where I live, to the neighbouring Town of Mont Royal (TMR), where my son attends elementary school. It is only a fifteen-minute walk, yet each day, passing through the fence feels a little like trespassing into another world. It seems that many others share my feelings of unease, for almost as soon as the Fence was built, it was subject to controversy.

The Fence was erected in June of 1960 by the TMR council, who had been petitioned by residents worried for their children's safety on the busy Acadie Boulevard (Di Cintio 2011). Later that year, an article dated December 20th 1960 appeared in the *Montreal Star*, describing a letter sent to TMR from the City of Montreal. The letter asks that the fence be removed as "the citizens of Montreal have been greatly offended" by its "unsightly" appearance (Gravenor 2007). Marcello di Cintio, in his article "The Great Wall of Montreal," details further controversies: A group of 300 students from the Université de Montréal, in 1971, tried to pull the fence down with their cars; the Fence gates were padlocked every Hallowe'en, a practice that began in the 1990s and stopped only in 2002. "The barrier has been referred to as 'apartheid fencing' and 'Montreal's Berlin Wall.'" notes di Cintio (di Cintio 2011, 1). This statement is a little hyperbolic, perhaps, for there are no guards, no barbed wire. Yet, it seems obvious enough to see the Fence as a symbol of division between the rich and the poor, given the contrasts between the neighbourhoods on either side. How is this symbol thus constructed? Would it be the same symbol if it were made from another material? What else might be said about it?

As I began to think about the Fence as a spatial dimension of history and social relations, I began to look at the Fence, literally, physically, through the lens of my camera. In photographing the entire fence during different times and seasons, the focusing, framing, editing, and compositing all became tools to explore the materiality of the fence itself. Over a two year period, I began to document the flowering of the hedge and the shedding of its leaves, how the wire of the fence was rusting in places, sagging, or newly patched, how snow drifted and was piled up against the fence in winter. The resulting photographic collage works as an archive of my journeys along and through the Fence, as well as the two neighbourhoods on either side; it makes no attempt to present a unified perspective, illustrating the multi-faceted nature of urban sites, especially controversial ones.

Looking for Thirdspace

Around the same time that I began photographing the Fence in 2011, I was also reading Edward Soja's *Thirdspace: Journeys to Los Angeles and Other Real-and-Imagined Places* (1996), which opened up many ways to approach a cultural reading of the Fence. Soja begins his influential book by stating a simple goal: to encourage a different way of seeing and thinking about "the spatiality of human life" in all its forms (Soja 1996, 1). He advocates a trialectical approach, based on Henri Lefebvre's theories in *The Production of Space,* which would take into equal account the three elements of spatiality, historicality, and sociality. Soja's three spaces correspond roughly to these three elements: 'Firstspace' focuses on the real, the visual, the material and the spatial, which is produced through the social; 'Secondspace' tends to be the most influential space, that of history and the imagined. As Lefebvre argues, "this is the dominant space in any society (or mode of production)" and tends towards language, text, discourse, and thus representations of ideology (quoted in Soja 1996, 67). 'Thirdspace' is what Soja calls the real-and-imagined, containing both First- and Second-spaces, but with an emphasis on social relations, power dynamics, lived experience, emotion, and the everyday (Ibid, 66-68).

In part two of the book, Soja begins to apply his approach to journeys (or case studies) through Los Angeles and Amsterdam. Los Angeles, he argues, is especially in need of different ways of seeing, with its problems of racial tension, class oppression, and other associated human inequalities. Soja focuses especially on the explosive Rodney King riots in 1992, relating the violence to the downtown spaces of LA and their histories. In contrast to the dystopia of LA, Amsterdam is presented as a city that works. His 'tourist' accounts of his journeys focus on ways of reading the landscape visually as well as historically, with an emphasis on the vernacular, the mundane and the everyday, and in this, Soja has much in common with writers in the field of cultural landscape theory.

This project on the Acadie Fence, both photographic collage and essay, takes its cue from Soja then, as well as others who focus on personal experiences of space, history, and social relations. I remain engaged with Soja's subjective approach, as well as Jackson's and Salmon's, both of whom emphasize the importance of individual knowledge. The following paper thus looks at the Fence through Soja's Three Spaces, first as a historical site, then as a material and cultural object produced by social space, and finally, as a real-and-imagined place with potential for resistance against its perceived function as a divisive barrier between the rich and the poor.

A Tale of Two Neighbourhoods (a Secondspace Analysis)

The rusty chain-link fence runs along Acadie Boulevard, nearly the entire length of the two neighbourhoods, hidden by a green and leafy hedge in the summer, exposed through the bare branches in the winter. It is about two metres high, approximately 1.6 kilometres long, and has only six gates, not necessarily located at the street intersections where one might think would be the logical spot for an opening. This fence was constructed in 1960, and has separated two neighbourhoods for over fifty years. But the two neighbourhoods on either side are a study in contrast in themselves, one being a middle class, suburban enclave, the other a densely populated immigrant ghetto. It could be said the fence simply spatializes the divisions that are already there.

In order to understand these divisions, one needs to have a basic understanding of their histories. We begin in Secondspace, then, with the dominant discourse of history, and with design and urban planning. We need to consider the past and its impact on the present. Thus, a Secondspace analysis would trace the development of these two neighbourhoods, one as a designed and planned model city specifically for the middle-class, the other as a real-estate company development selling to working-class families. These two different histories reflect the impact of design, urban planning, and imagination ('the conceived') on the built environment.

TMR has an especially well-documented history as one of Canada's first experiments in urban planning. L.D. McCann's article "Planning and building the corporate suburb of Mount Royal, 1910–1925" (1996) outlines the history of TMR as designed by Frederic Gage Todd (1876–1948), a disciple of Frederick Law Olmsted, and considered to be Canada's first landscape architect. Todd modeled the design of TMR according to Olmsted's City Beautiful ideas, and was influenced as well by the Garden City and Garden Suburb movements, all of which emphasized the importance of architecture and urban planning to promote a harmonious social order through beautification and greenery.

TMR was also conceived as a model city on the initiative of the Canadian Northern Railway, and this is reflected throughout the town's architecture and street names. McCann notes that in TMR, as in other affluent Montreal neighbourhoods such as Westmount and Outremont, builders began to respond to a demand for singlespring owner-occupied, detached residences that saw a clear break with the renter-occupied row housing that defined the rest of urban Montreal (McCann 1996, 260-263).

Contrasted with the highly-planned and relatively exclusive nature of TMR, Parc-X developed as part of the housing boom that occurred with the expansion of Montreal in the years prior to the First World War. Pierre Brassard, in "Les origines de Parc-Extension," gives an account of how the area was converted from farmland, divided into small lots by real estate speculators, and sold to families of modest income. The neighbourhood grew slowly at first, then after the construction of the Jean-Talon railway station (Park Avenue station) in 1931, it developed rapidly to accommodate workers of the factories that had been established nearby. Parc-X is one of the poorest and most diverse neighbourhoods in Montreal, with one of the highest population densities, and has been home to wave after wave of immigrant influx. Brassard writes that Parc-X is in transition from an identity as Little Greece to the more recent identity as Little India, although there are also many residents from Ghana, Vietnam, Turkey, Sri Lanka, Pakistan, and Bangladesh (Brassard 2010, 1-3).

The histories of these two neighbourhoods show that they both developed according to specific ideas around the spatialization of class. For instance, the row housing and tight grid of Parc-X continued the pattern set in Montreal's urban areas, especially the working-class neighbourhoods in the central and eastern parts of the city. In contrast, TMR was designed as an attempt to manifest the middle-class suburban ideal, to break away from the city grid and to incorporate "curving streets, spacious lots, small parks, and other countryside amenities – all radical features at the time" (McCann 1996, 276). Although much of TMR is actually a looser, modified grid, the two diagonals that slice across the town and meet at the center, and the series of cul-de-sacs at the edges, contribute to the impression that TMR is built on curves, in contrast with the tight grid on which the rest of the city is built (McCann 1996, 260-263).

The grid versus curves dichotomy illustrates how urban planning shapes the social atmosphere of each neighbourhood. The grid, championed by Jackson as "one of the most ambitious schemes in history for the orderly creation of landscapes, of small communities," (Jackson 1980, 115-116) organizes space efficiently. Jackson further enumerated the ways the grid system allows for flexibility and interchangeability in its usage of space, which helps to contribute to the development of the mixed-usage neighbourhoods that advocates of New Urbanism so often praise (Jacobs 1961). Indeed, Parc-X has many restaurants, bakeries, depanneurs, churches and other amenities, all in walking distance of each other. The high population density also contributes to a very social atmosphere, and, at times, friction among its very heterogeneous residents.[1]

Curves, on the other hand, as a manifestation of the suburban ideal, work to present an oasis in contrast with the rest of the city. The wide lawns and hedges in place of fences contribute to the appearance of flowing green space that is widely associated with the upper-middle class suburb (Jurkow 2000, 5). In TMR, the low population density means that chance meetings with strangers are rare. Because residential areas are separate from service areas, TMR residents rely on their cars. There are no metro stops within TMR borders and bus service is poor. There are no depanneurs or any other commercial businesses in walking distance, unless one lives close to the center or its outer edges. But because there is little traffic on its winding streets, the neighbourhood is a great place for strolling, jogging, and biking, although it is very easy to get lost. The cul-de-sacs strewn along the edges of the town make for a disorienting, confusing exploration, and of course, as this is part of their function, to discourage traffic. They also work along with other elements of 'taste regulation' (lawn maintenance, architectural restrictions, and other such by-laws), which discourage diversity in income groups, making for a more homogenous community (Low 2006, 87).

I could continue to enumerate the differences between TMR and Parc-X, but this project is not wholly about the differences, but rather their manifestation as a fence. For now, suffice it to say that different approaches to urban planning resulted in neighbourhoods that have spatialized class relations in the layout of the streets and in the architecture. This in turn influenced and influences the different social spaces of the two neighbourhoods. These same elements influence what the Fence is, through its materials and its significance.

Looking at the Fence (A Firstspace Analysis)

Cultural landscape studies, with its emphasis on the visual and material, provide a solid basis for a Firstspace investigation ('the perceived'). Indeed, the material acts as a manifestation of the social, and provides us with a methodology of reading urban sites. What are some of the different ways of reading the Fence? What does the Fence say about social relations, and how?

In her landmark essay of 1915, "History in a Back Yard," Lucy Salmon offered a typology of fences. She looked at the associations built into different kinds of fences, the materials, and the reasons for being built. For example, she wrote that if

> A high hedge is selected to mark the boundary lines, it suggests not only a love of retirement and contemplation, but a desire for protection from dust… it also renders a secondary service of beauty scarcely less important than its primary one of indicating boundary lines. But, after all, wall and fence and hedge are but outward symbols of a crude method of marking private ownership (Salmon 2001, 77-78).

What do the fence and hedge say here, and how do they manifest Secondspace history?

Frame 1: The Hedge

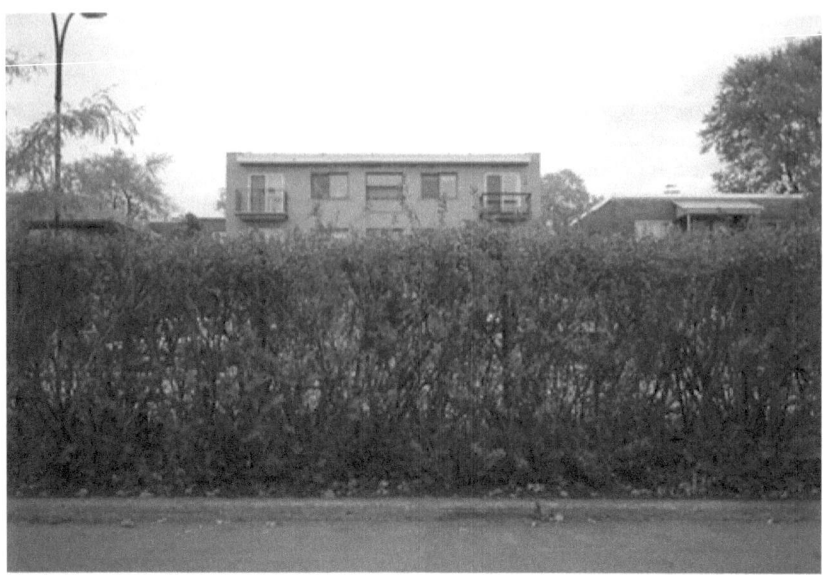

Acadie Fence - Hedge. TAIEN NG-CHAN. 2011. Courtesy of the artist.

Because of the hedge, the Fence is not always immediately visible. The hedge grows on both sides of it, which, as Salmon purported, helps to screen out dust and dirt flying up from the traffic on Acadie, and also hides the fence itself, which is made of wire. The hedge suggests the need to beautify what would otherwise be unsightly. And indeed, this view is supported by this quote from *La Presse*, dated January 18th, 1962 (translated):

> Prominent people in the Town of Mount Royal, including Mayor Reginald Dawson, have started to regret the famous fence which divides the east side of the city along Acadie Boulevard. At a landlord association meeting of the independent municipality… Mr. William Tetley said that "everywhere we go in Montreal they talk to us about the fence." He added that the wall is a terrible symbol. As a result he proposes that the height of the fence be reduced from six to three feet and that it be pulled back two feet within the city limits and that it be hidden by bushes (Gravenor 2007).

This comment begs the question, if the fence needed to be hidden, then why have a fence at all? Would a hedge on its own not be enough? Certainly it would serve the same purpose of protection and demarcation. One answer might be that a hedge cannot serve as a gate.

Frame 2: Gates

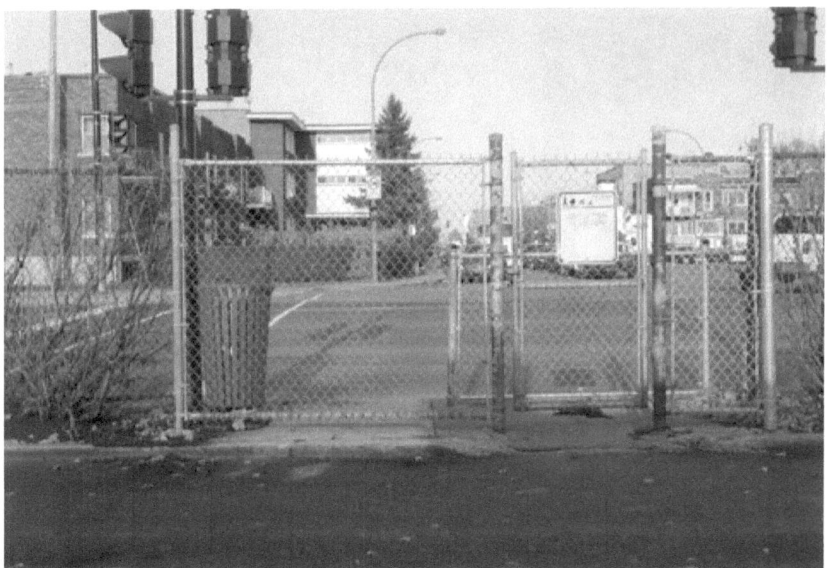

Acadie Fence – Gates at Jarry. TAIEN NG-CHAN. 2011. Courtesy of the artist.

Let us take a closer look at the gates in the Fence, the only points of access between the two neighbourhoods along Acadie Boulevard. The gates are located near Rue de Liege on its northern end and Rue Jean-Talon at its southern end, at the Parc-X intersections of Jarry, St-Roch, and Olgivy, and one – seemingly randomly – in between Olgivy and St-Roch. The two remaining intersections at Avenue Ball and at Avenue d'Anvers do not have gates, probably because there are no pedestrian crosswalks here. More access points would certainly be welcome though. When the Fence was first built, there was only one pedestrian opening, and more gates were added through the years (di Cintio 2011). In addition, the gate at major intersection of Rue Jarry is the only one that features a cage-like structure, making it more difficult for bicycles to pass through. All the gates are rusty and heavy, constructed from wire and steel posts, and they clang loudly when they swing shut. They are not what I would call friendly.

Frame 3: A Hole in the Fence

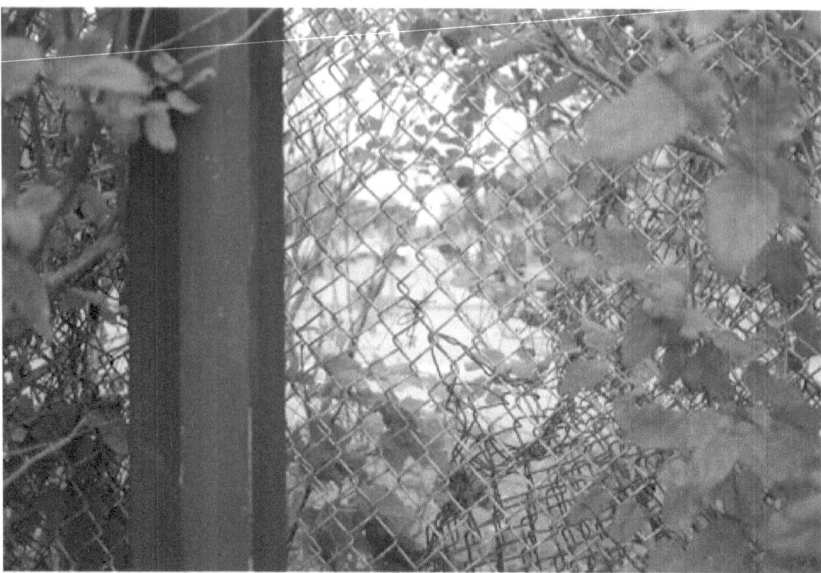

Acadie Fence – A Hole in the Fence. TAIEN NG-CHAN. 2011. Courtesy of the artist.

Although there is no gate in the Fence at the intersection of Ball and Acadie, it seems that there should be. There are no stoplights or crosswalks here, or at Avenue d'Anvers (the only other intersection without a gate), but some people cross anyways, hurrying across the four lanes of busy traffic. Montreal is a city where jaywalking is a normal part of pedestrian culture. It seems natural that someone, wanting to cross the Fence at Avenue Ball, rather than having to walk the long block up to the gate at Jarry or down to St-Roch, would cut a hole in the fence. This hole at Ball is the only one that I can detect, the only challenge to the fence's control of access. But the hole is patched up now, and so far, no further attempts have been made to open it (unlike the ongoing battles further south at the Mile End railway crossings, where that fence has been cut and patched innumerable times and in several different spots).[2] If the hole in the Acadie Fence were to be made bigger, or opened again and again, would the authorities finally put in a gate? What challenges can affect the materialities of the Fence? There does not seem to be the same willpower or need here as in Mile End, where people are more politically engaged with the urban landscape. Here, the quiet challenge of a hole in the fence can go almost unnoticed.

Frame 4: Signs

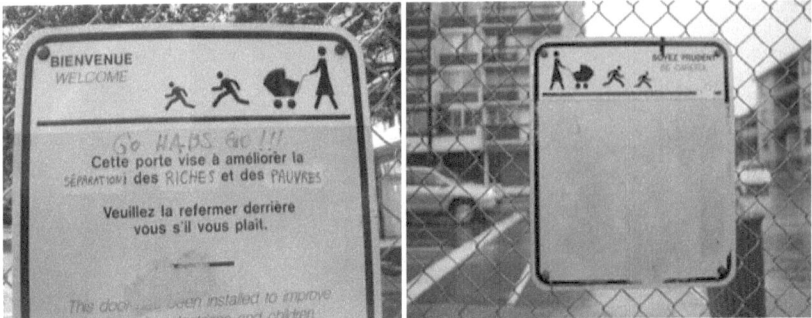

Acadie Fence – Gate Signs. TAIEN NG-CHAN. 2011. Courtesy of the artist.

There are signs on both sides of the gate. Going into TMR, the sign, in English and French, says, "Welcome. This door has been installed to improve safety of pedestrians and children. Please make sure you close it after you. Town of Mont Royal." On leaving TMR, the sign says the same thing, but instead of "Welcome," it says simply, "Be Careful." This posits the interior of TMR as a safe space, the exterior as filled with various dangers, the busy boulevard being only one of many. People have taken issue with this, attacking the signs themselves through graffiti and general defacement, usually to the sign that warns "Be Careful." The dichotomy between the two sides of the signs belies the stated intention of simple protection (from what, exactly, is not stated). It enforces instead the perceived view of the Fence as a barrier to separate the rich from the poor, as seen in the alterations to one particular sign pictured above (which was cleaned up within days of its appearance).

Frame 5: Empty

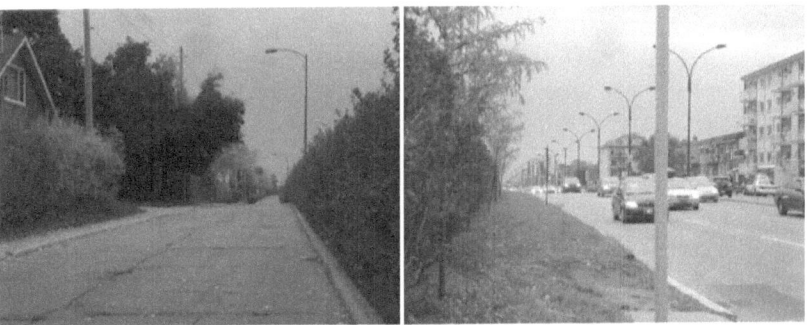

Acadie Fence – On Both Sides. TAIEN NG-CHAN. 2011. Courtesy of the artist.

During a year and a half of almost daily walks to and from TMR, never once have I seen children playing on the streets near the Fence. Indeed, the street closest to the fence in TMR functions as a cushion to block the sights and sounds of Acadie Boulevard. Nothing is located there. No houses actually face this street or the fence. There are only back yards and side yards, each with their own fence or hedge. Sometimes I glimpse swimming pools through the back yard fences, though they seem rarely used. I sometimes see landscapers tending to gardens, mothers and strollers out for a walk, joggers, or groups of high school kids after school. Usually, however, the streets are empty. Where are the people that the Fence is protecting?

Frame 6: Where the Sidewalk Ends

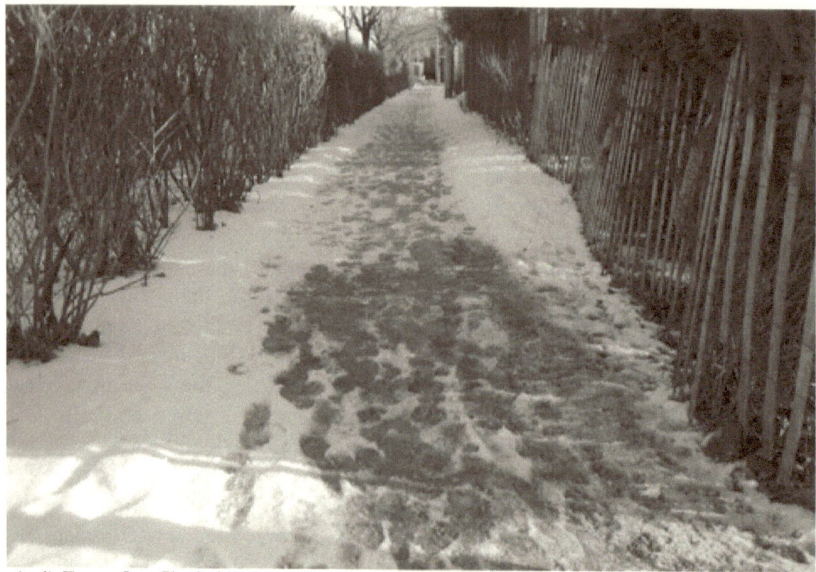

Acadie Fence – Snow Tracks. TAIEN NG-CHAN. 2012. Courtesy of the artist.

The street and sidewalk curve away here, but there is a dirt path worn in, visible even more in the snow. These are the footprints of people headed to and from Metro Acadie, just outside the TMR borders. These patterns of circulation show what is important to those who use the landscape, especially pedestrians and cyclists, and what the urban planners have ignored (Moskowitz 2009, 74).

Frame 7: Places for Padlocks

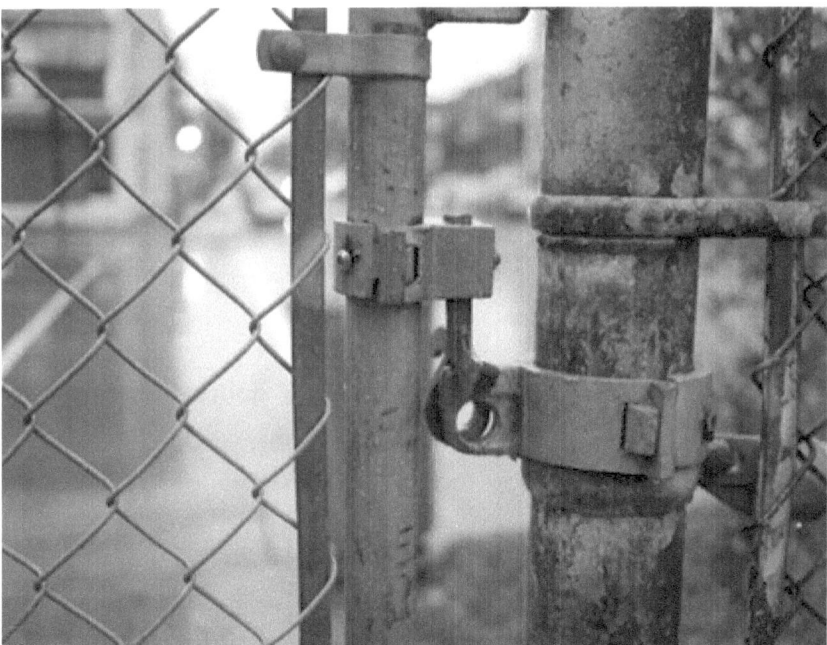

Acadie Fence – Places for Padlocks. TAIEN NG-CHAN. 2011. Courtesy of the artist.

The question is, why would a fence such as this ever need to be locked? To lock out. On Hallowe'en, for instance. From the 1990s until 2002, the Acadie Fence was padlocked every year on Hallowe'en night, ostensibly to discourage Parc-X children from trick-or-treating or vandalizing in TMR, all in the name of 'protection' (di Cintio 2011). This highlights the use of 'protection' as a discourse to delimit the boundaries of public spaces and their usage. Rosalyn Deutsche, in her essay 'Agoraphobia' (1996), used a singular example to illustrate how 'public' is not an all-inclusive term. She examined a story that was run in 1991 in the *New York Times* (Roberts 1991) about a small public park in Greenwich Village, its rehabilitation from dilapidation, and its subsequent padlocking at night to keep out the homeless. Jackson Park, the little plaza at the center of the story, became the focus of an upper-middle class neighbourhood group, "Friends of Jackson Park," which was welcomed by the City Parks Department as 'public' help in "protecting public space" (Deutsche 1996, 276). Through this example, Deutsche argued that the term 'public' does not include the economically disadvantaged.

There are pertinent parallels between the padlocking of Jackson Square and the Acadie Fence, both as 'protective' measures. TMR officials basically defined Parc-X kids as vandals while TMR kids were not. In effect, Parc-X children were also discouraged from trick-or-treating in the wealthier neighbourhood. Hallowe'en is not an especially popular holiday in Parc-X, perhaps because it is not a custom with the many immigrant populations residing there. Only a few houses are ever decorated, whereas in TMR, on each street immediately adjacent to Acadie

Boulevard, there are several houses with at times rather impressive Hallowe'en displays, indicating participation in the yearly ritual of trick-or-treating. It seems natural that kids would want to cross over to TMR, and in the past, they simply went around the padlocked Fence (di Cintio 2011). Though the Fence's gates are no longer padlocked on Hallowe'en, the past lingers in the public's memory. Many of the parents with small children in Parc-X do consider crossing over to TMR now, though in conversation, some of them have expressed their feelings that they were "unwanted" in that neighbourhood, and that perhaps they would just stay in Parc-X. The locks are the focal point of the Fence's symbolism, the one feature that says most clearly how divisive it is, all in the name of 'protection.'

Counterspaces (a Thirdspace conclusion)

Many city councillors on both sides of the Fence, as well as one TMR mayor, have wanted to take the Fence down, but still it stands. As Jackson noted, fences are often used to derive identity from a shared landscape, to maintain a view of inner suburban cohesion against the outsider, against the city (Cited in Moskowitz 2009, 74). Indeed, the 'Townies,' as TMR residents are known as colloquially, seem to have no problem with the Fence. The gates were removed in 2002 after the Hallowe'en padlocking became a scandal, but were reinstated in 2005 after demands were made at Town Council. Pierre Bourque, mayor of Montreal from 1994 to 2001, observed that "the people of TMR seem to have some sort of psychological need" for the Fence (di Cintio 2011, 2). Whether this psychological need pertains to so-called safety or protection issues, or to deep-seated fears and prejudices against the economically disadvantaged, is in the end irrelevant. The perceived function of the Fence, as read through its history and its materiality, has marked the urban landscape emotionally as a symbol of discrimination.

But boundaries are not always marked with fences. For example, Parc-X and TMR are within the same school zone, the borders of which are drawn up by the English Montreal School Board (EMSB), and this is the reason that I encounter the Fence almost daily. The school zone therefore brings certain residents of TMR and Parc-X together, resulting in contact that would otherwise not occur. This contact remains based in the politics of language, for only people who fit the rather narrow criteria of the EMSB are permitted access to English schools. Under Quebec law, immigrants from any country, even English speaking ones such as the United States, must attend French schools. This means that the great diversity of Parc-X is filtered out to a large extent. Thus, although the school zone boundaries are broad enough to suggest possibilities of engagement across the Fence, in my experience, this contact has been relatively superficial, perhaps because of other factors such as class and income. These sociological considerations, however interesting, take us beyond the space of this essay.

School zone boundaries provide suggestions into how we can read the different functions of borders, and how we might imagine other ways to view the Acadie Fence. A space of the real-and-imagined offers a view beyond the binary. In a Thirdspace analysis, spatiality and historicity combine with sociality to find a politically charged edge, and a way to perhaps engage and effect social change. Here is the space that takes into account the direct experiences of everyday life, and the space that questions and challenges power dynamics. Soja also placed art here, where the real and imagined, or "things and thought," are on equal terms, making the space fertile for the growth of counterspaces, "spaces of resistance to the dominant order arising precisely from their subordinate, peripheral or marginalized positioning" (Soja 1996, 68). There is a strong activist element underlying Soja's formulations of Thirdspace.

What kinds of actions might make the Fence more visible through its camouflage of hedge, to engage it in Thirdspace? The graffiti and defacements to the signs are one form of challenge, as is the hole in the Fence. Art can certainly act as another challenge, perhaps through such practices as yarn-bombing and guerilla signage. Although I have not seen instances of such artistic challenge on the Fence itself, they have occurred around other sites in Parc-X and indicate the possibilities. With the photo-collage of the Fence, I also hope to open up another space, where the everyday familiar is made strange, and where social and material history become evident in everyday life.

Imagine if the wire and steel posts were taken down. The hedges could remain to provide the sense of safety that TMR residents obviously seek. But the rusty metal doors, which are long overdue for maintenance, could be replaced by, say, wooden gates, perhaps painted a dark green to form a continuous flow with the hedge. There would not and should not be padlocks on the gates because these neighbourhoods themselves are not private property. These are just some suggestions towards (re)envisioning the Fence that takes into account the larger borders and the different boundaries that join the two neighbourhoods, rather than divide them. Parc-X is open to TMR for all of its amenities, its many restaurants, and its dépanneurs. TMR is a green space for Parc-X. Neighbours should share the neighbourhood, because we are, after all, neighbours.

Fired Ground: Warsaw's History in Brick

Samantha Oswald

Fired Ground: Warsaw's History in Brick

Samantha Oswald

It is well-known that writing the history of a war-torn country is normally a privilege of the victors. At first glance, the skyline of Warsaw, Poland attests to that fact. The 230m tall Palace of Culture and Science, a gift from Joseph Stalin, still presides over the socialist housing estates and the glass-and-steel skyscrapers that have come to constellate around it. At ground level, though, hidden beneath layers of plaster or tucked as ruins between larger buildings, a different story begins to emerge, one in which the humble brick, the base unit of construction for much of Warsaw's history, takes on the role of protagonist. Telling Warsaw's story through an examination of brick allows the full complexity of its multiple historical narratives to emerge, since at different points in time, brick has come to stand for contradicting concepts: freedom and oppression, solidity and ruin, humanization and monotony, and legislation and self-organization.

Unlike the monumentality of concrete slabs and sheets of glass, the fine-grained texture of brick is in constant flux, deconstructed and reconstructed, never entirely completed and never entirely erased. Brick's scale, mobility, and interchangeability allow it to acquire value. This value, however, is not always economic. It can also be political, mnemonic, and social. As an icon, as an item, and as a record of labour and energy, this often-ignored object acts as a currency of meaning in the built environment.

Skyline and Groundline

> After the fire of 1431 which destroyed the town, the Town Council ordered that no wooden dwellings be erected thereafter. Thus Warsaw was rebuilt of red brick... (Ciborowski 1964, 14)

Although, chronologically, this is where the story of brick in Warsaw begins, the relevance of chronology is questionable in a city that was rebuilt in the 1950s looking exactly as it did in the 1750s. It is more productive to examine the city as it is experienced: as the locus of unexpected juxtapositions, eloquent surfaces, and barely repressed histories.

Mid-town Warsaw is unapologetically consumerist. Perhaps trying to compensate for almost half a century of closed borders and a state-run economy, it gleefully announces on every possible surface its participation in the global market. The platonic forms and textureless planes of modernist towers prove to be ideal for projection, willingly accepting any character bestowed upon them by photographs of swimsuited models and sleek cars. This is the skyline of the city: meant to be observed from afar.

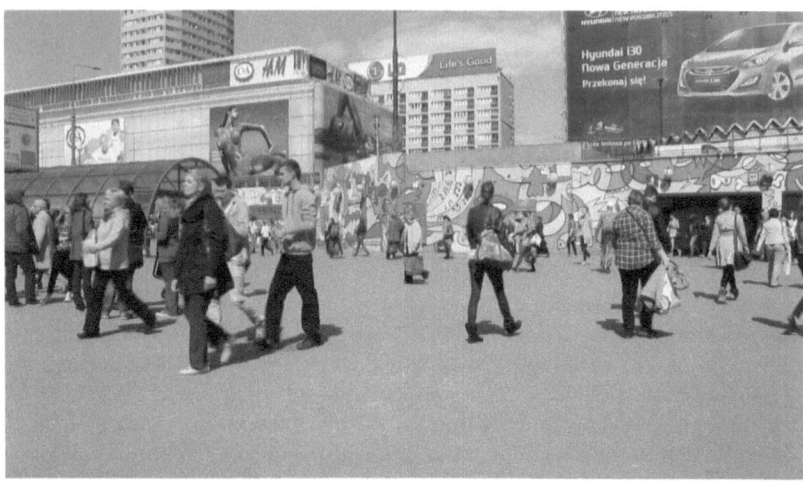

Mid-town Warsaw. Photograph by author.

Approaching this mask of advertisements dissolves them into meaningless pixels, and the initial dazzlement is replaced by the gritty reality of an urban collage. Fragments of the nineteenth century industrial city exist as leftovers sandwiched between glass office blocks and socialist housing. Tenement houses with sombre courtyards wait patiently for their saviours or more likely their destroyers all the while inexorably falling into ruin. Most have a skirt of netting suspended just above the ground floor to prevent the crumbling brick from dropping onto unsuspecting pedestrians. On one hand, they are a blight on the glossy face with which Warsaw would like to present itself and on the other, simply by existing, they are inadvertent monuments. They have survived the war, in some cases both world wars. No small accomplishment in a city that was 85% rubble in 1944.[3]

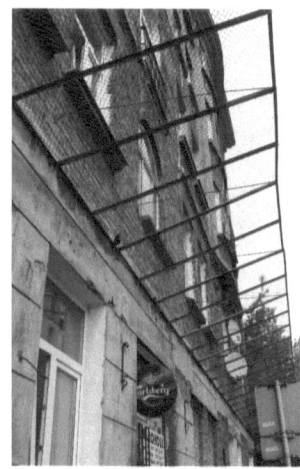

The contested position of these buildings in the city fabric is not unnoticed by artists and architects. A large mural covering the bare expanse of brick at 14 Walicow street poses the question succinctly: kamien i co? The words are a pun; taken together, kamienico means 'apartment house', and separated, the

Crumbling brick is caught by netting. Photograph by author.

phrase becomes 'stone and what?' Are these houses meaningful pieces of Warsaw's heritage? Or are they simply hovels, waiting to be bulldozed to make room for the image-city?

Their physical reality is often deplorable. The courtyards receive very little light, and the uninsulated brick walls are an energy drain in the cold Polish climate. If the brick was covered by a layer of render, the crumbling plaster reveals sloppily executed construction, and if brick was also used for facing, it spalls. These conditions have led to the perception of these tenements as slums, a perception that is linked to their material.

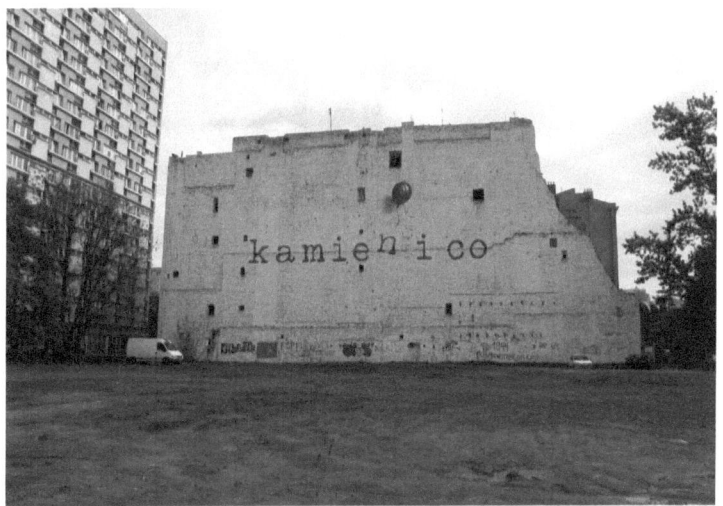

The mural at Ulica Waliców 14. Photograph by author.

Nowhere is this stigma more apparent than in the district of Praga. Located on the east bank of the Vistula river, opposite the downtown core, it is one of the rare neighbourhoods which was not destroyed during the Second World War. Here, the buildings are caught in a tension between speculation, good intentions on the part of the municipality, and the notoriously surly current inhabitants:

> With the fall of communism it seemed that the neighbourhood, a 15-minute tram ride from the city centre, must modernise. However, this has not yet happened. First, unusually in the context of a city reconstructed after World War II, a significant amount of Praga's architectural infrastructure is listed as heritage sites which would-be developers are required to preserve and revitalise. These regulations, together with the serious disrepair of many of the buildings, have combined to dissuade investors principally interested in locations for cheap and easy construction. Secondly, many of the tenement buildings are subject to complex ownership issues, in some cases involving restitution to the inheritors of pre-war proprietors. And thirdly, the local population has a reputation for social pathology (Cope 2010, 106).

Praga's brick tenements are a vestige of the living conditions associated with the nineteenth century industrial city. They were constructed cheaply as housing for the workers of the factories, and were often overcrowded and unsanitary (Ciborowski 1964, 20). They retain their blue-collar ethos even as they are slowly abandoned.

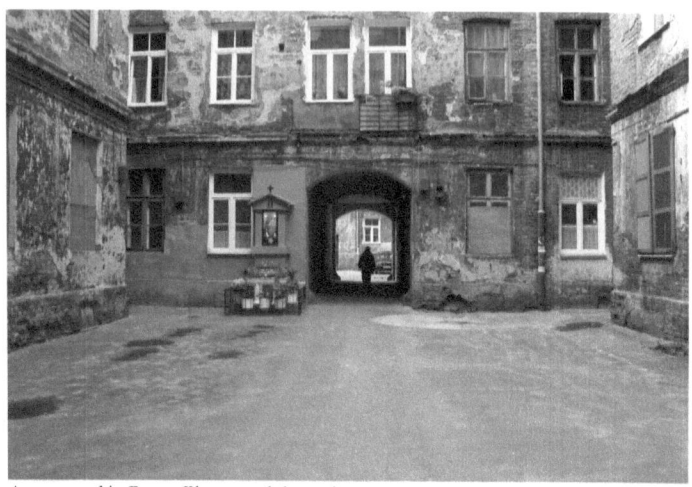

A courtyard in Praga. Photograph by author.

The factories that employed these labourers were also built of the same material, but they were durably constructed and maintained, out of necessity, by their respective companies. As a result, some of the most poignant spaces of Warsaw's industrial heritage are crafted of finely detailed brick. Some of these remain abandoned, but the high quality of construction has made them targets for developers seeking to market their raw aesthetic for loft living and cultural events. Brick, in this case, increases their value. The adaptive reuse of industrial brick buildings has become highly fashionable, as manifested by projects such as Herzog and de Meuron's conversion of the Bankside power station in London to the Evergreen Brickworks complex in Toronto.

The Koneser vodka factory occupies a prominent position in the heart of Praga, and is currently the site of a €97.8 million investment[4] to convert it into a complex with "centres of culture, luxury lofts, modern office buildings and retail and service premises."[5] In its present state, though, partially demolished, mostly abandoned, it testifies to

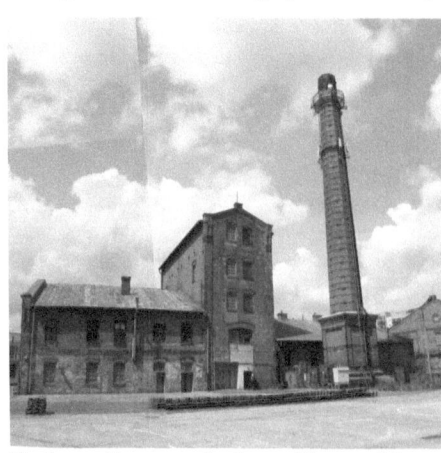

The former Koneser vodka factory. Photograph by author.

the ambiguity between industrial no-man's-land and space for cutting-edge grunge culture. A theatre and gallery occupy two different corners of the site, and it is not

uncommon to be the only visitor, wandering under the scrutiny of the security guard at the front gate. Whether these independent operations will survive the renovation and its corresponding increase in rent is unclear. Around them, piles of bricks from demolitions grow steadily higher.

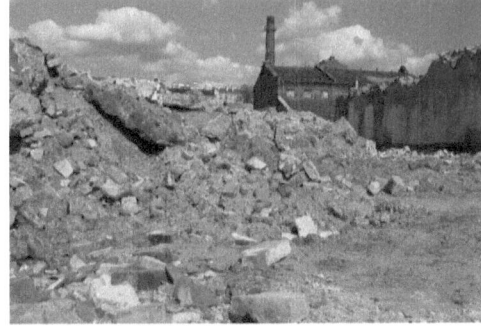

Demolitions behind the Koneser factory. Photograph by author.

Rubble and Relic

The association of brick with ruin is also employed deliberately to evoke the events of the Second World War. At that time, partially collapsed brick walls were a daily reality for Varsovians, since their city was damaged by successive attacks and air raids. The Nazi occupiers responded to any kind of resistance with the destruction of the built fabric. This occurred during the initial siege of Warsaw in 1939, the eradication of the Jewish Ghetto in 1943, and the Warsaw Uprising of 1944 (Tung 2001, 74). Since then, collapsing brick has gained the status of icon: detached from its original context, it is cast in metal, drawn as an image, or preserved in its ruined state as memorials to the Poles' fight for freedom.

Whereas 'brick' as it refers to the Uprising is treated as an abstract and non-specific symbol, the remaining fragments of the Jewish ghetto wall have acquired individual significance to the point of becoming relics. The pieces of wall figure on tourist maps and on the itineraries of Jewish tour groups who come to pay their respects, sometimes leaving tokens for their murdered compatriots. The bricks of the wall gain a sanctity and authenticity from their location. Some are even relocated to Jewish history museums around the world.

The Warsaw Ghetto of the Second World War was the largest in Europe, and had an area of 3.7 square kilometres and a perimeter of over 20 kilometres.[6] Although existing buildings were incorporated into the perimeter as much as possible, often brick walls of 3 metres, topped by 1 metre of barbed wire, were constructed to ensure continuity. In 1943, as the Nazis commenced implementation of the 'final solution', the inhabitants of the

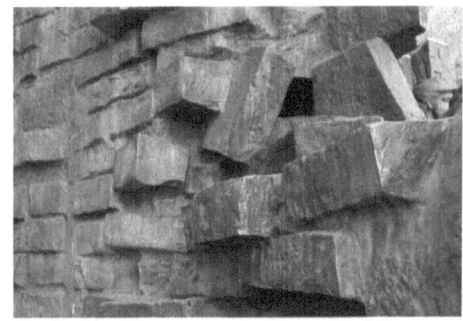

Detail of the Monument to the Warsaw Uprising. Photograph by author.

ghetto, against overwhelming odds, fought against their oppressors for almost a month (Tung 2001, 78). As punishment, the entire area was reduced to rubble (Ibid).

> With armed troops in attendance to act as execution squads, the ghetto was razed structure by structure. Afterwards, bulldozers pulverized and levelled the broken pieces. The Germans had in effect erased an urban area of about one square mile. No buildings remained, no sidewalks, no streets, no green—just a field of shards (Tung 2001, 78-79).

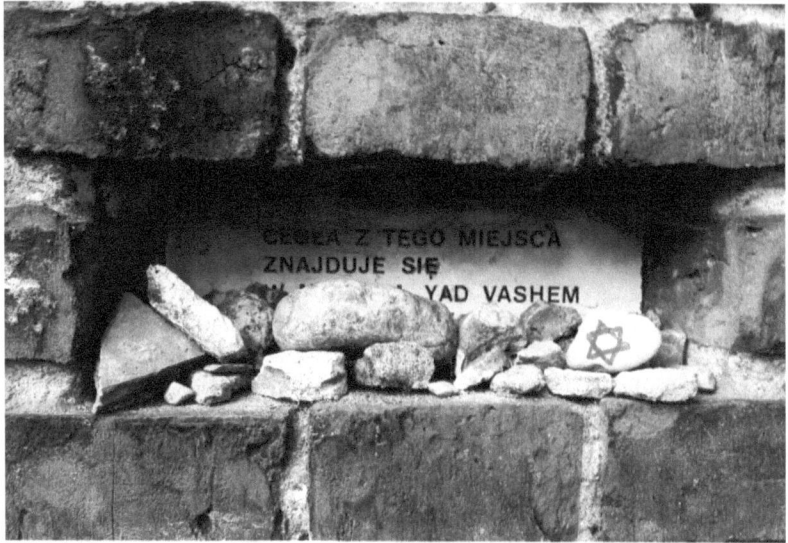

This brick has been removed for preservation in the Yad Vashem centre, Israel. Photograph by author.

Given the ubiquity of brick both during and after the war, it is simply by chance that these particular bricks of the ghetto wall have survived to acquire the status of artefacts. In that sense, they are both specific and symbolic: they come from a particular place, yet they are made to stand for the persecution and loss of freedom experienced by the entire Jewish population during the Holocaust.

The devastation wrought in the ghetto was repeated a few months later in the rest of the city. At the end of 1944, the Nazis commenced a systematic annihilation of all of Warsaw's built heritage (Tung 2001, 81). Specially named detachments placed explosives at key structural points of buildings, ensuring that their collapse would be complete (Ibid.). The territory of the city became a landscape, a topography of millions of bricks.

As soon as the Germans left the city, displaced Poles started to return, despite the fact that their homes were unrecognizable. They started to clear the streets, sorting the rubble for reuse. As a community, they started to rebuild.

Cities, like people, are born with a soul, a spirit of place that continues to make itself known, emerging even after devastation, an old word looking for meaning in the new mouth that speaks it. For though there were no buildings left and there was waste farther than the horizon, Warsaw never stopped being a city (Michaels 2009, 214).

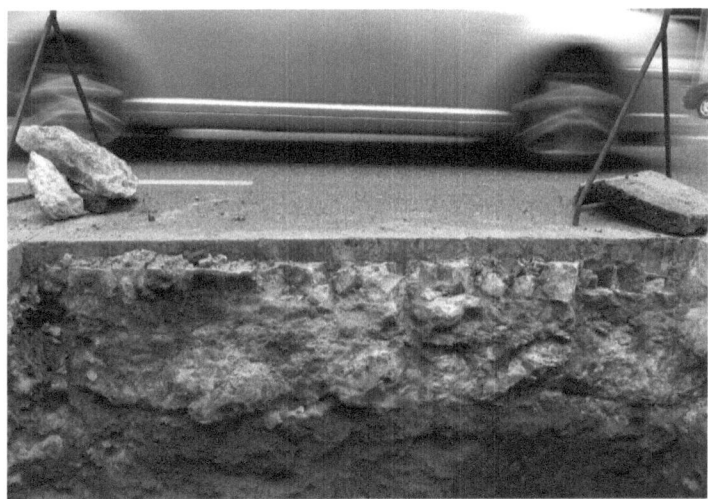

Warsaw's red underbelly. Photograph by author.

Brick is the only material that allowed for this self-organization. As a modular unit of a size that can easily be handled by one worker, and as discrete blocks that could be salvaged from the wreckage, brick allowed all citizens to contribute their labour to the reconstruction.

The Soviet government, which had taken power after the war, saw in the spontaneous rebuilding efforts a chance to gain legitimacy and acceptance among the Polish people (Crowley 1997, 203). They adopted an ambitious six-year plan for the reconstruction of Warsaw. The shortage of building materials available after the war, coupled with the accelerated schedule for reconstruction, resulted in an artificial inflation of the economic value of brick. Warsaw was meant to act as a showcase for the resilience and solidarity of the Polish people; as such, all resources went towards the capital (Thum 2011, 140).

Party writers sought to persuade the Poles to employ a new adjective in everyday speech. 'Varsovian' was to be used to describe extraordinary achievement (buildings were erected at warszawskie tempo- Varsovian tempo) (Crowley 1997, 209).

The collection, donation, and construction of bricks became a national activity. For many Poles, a trip to Warsaw to help with the reconstruction had the feel of a holiday, especially in the post-war jubilation (Crowley 1997, 208). The celebration of Warsaw masked the reality of brick harvesting in many lesser cities. In Wrocław, for example, many buildings with only minimal damage were deconstructed to send bricks to Warsaw (Thum 2011, 130). The exact form of the reconstruction was much debated, but the patriotism and sentimentality of the city's inhabitants dictated a replication, a return to 'how it was before'. Even once that was agreed upon, however, the question of the exact meaning of 'before' remained. For Warsaw, like many other European cities, had undergone numerous transformations over its 500-odd year history. The shabby pre-war state of its Stare Miasto and Nowe Miasto, (Old Town, originally 13th century, and New Town, originally fourteenth century[7]) would not do as the face of Poland's revival. Finally, the town planners settled on their Baroque incarnations, and paintings by Bernardo Bellotto of the city in 1779 were used as architectural documents.

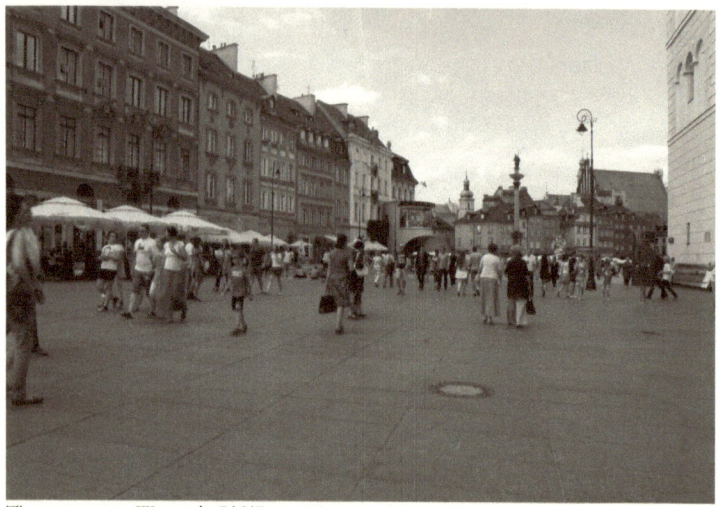

The entrance to Warsaw's Old Town. Photograph by author.

Aesthetic and Archaeology

The destruction unexpectedly benefited archaeologists and historians by exposing parts of buildings that had been subsumed by centuries of accreted constructions. Warsaw's Gothic persona and subsequent growth could be inferred by making detailed measurements, down to the millimetre, of the bricks in a particular wall. Using a graphic tool to map and compare sizes of bricks, historians identified which walls were constructed at the same time, using bricks from the same yard, and which bricks had been reused from previous constructions.[8]

Most of the facades in the Stare Miasto and Nowe Miasto were covered by a brightly painted layer of plaster. To simulate Warsaw's impromptu growth, however, the red brick – traces of the Gothic – was occasionally left exposed. For these errant fragments detailed drawings were made, laying out the position of each brick in the wall. This was for aesthetic reasons, but also for practicality, as a way to determine the amount of whole bricks needed, and where broken pieces could be used instead.[9]

Despite brick's importance as the currency and medium of Warsaw's reconstruction, it was almost always covered with a layer of render. Rendering allowed the walls to be erected quickly, using unskilled labour, and with mismatched and broken bricks. As well, the association of bricks with ruin pervaded the mentality of the Poles, who wanted nothing more than to see the face of their city smooth and unscarred. Adolf Ciborowski, writing in 1964 about Warsaw's efforts at reconstruction, laments:

> Unfortunately, raw, unfinished walls of red brick are still a prominent feature of the Warsaw landscape. They are left from the past, when bricks were the main building material in Warsaw; because of a shortage of skilled labour, outer walls of buildings were left unplastered and more buildings put up instead. These red blotches are now being gradually removed (Cibrowski 1964, 304).

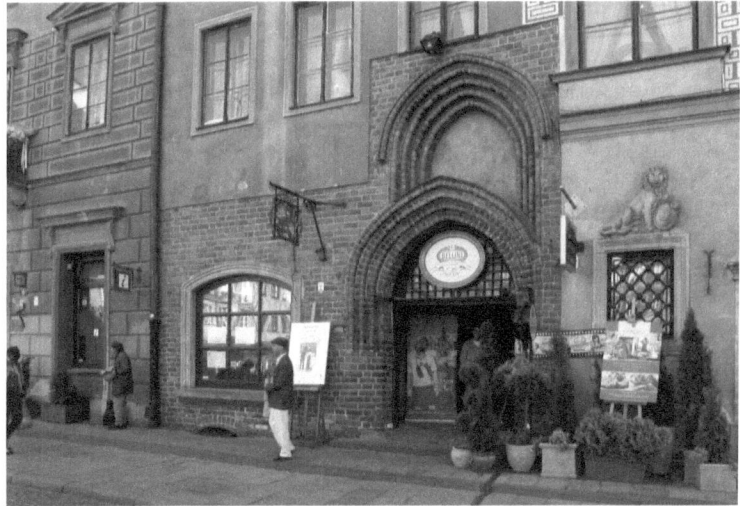

A Gothic portal in the old town. Photograph by author.

It is only red brick that acquires such disrepute, as Ciborowski goes on to state: "To prevent the reoccurence of such a situation in the future, grey calcium-silicate bricks have been in general use since 1958 for outer wall facing" (Ibid).

Grey brick was first used extensively in Warsaw in the mid 1920s, when the rejection of applied ornament initiated the transition to varied brickwork as a means of expression. Influenced by German and Dutch expressionism and Functionalism, grey brick was chosen as an affordable alternative to stone cladding, and was used for many institutional and residential projects. Its "capability to demonstrate prestige", however, was deemed too limited to make it suitable for higher-profile administrative buildings (Roguska 2009, 33). The 'grey-brick functionalist' style was considered characteristic of Warsaw and remained popular until the advent, around 1933, of a more reductive modernism following le Corbusier's five principles (Ibid).

Monotony and Humanity

The Soviets permitted sentimentality to dictate the reconstruction of the Stare Miasto and Nowe Miasto. In other parts of Warsaw, they undertook to create monumental squares and boulevards as symbols of Communist Poland (Crowley 1997, 208). These were designed in their chosen style of Social Realism, which made use of applied ornament as propaganda to forward the interests of the Party. Choosing the iconic properties of sculpture instead of the subtler, indexical nature of the brick walls, they immortalized the bricklayer in oversized statues while hiding his work beneath panels of stone. The nature of communist labour privileged quantity over quality, and the fastest teams of bricklayers were lauded in public ceremonies (Ibid). The romanticization of labour is evident in the art from that period: works such as the

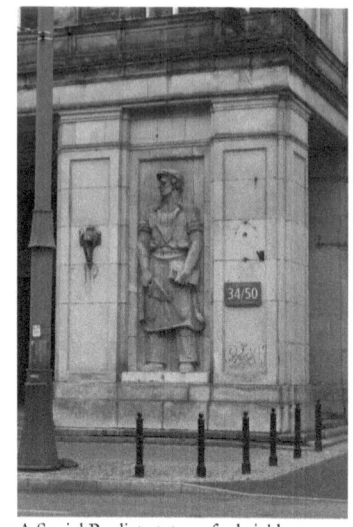

A Social Realist statue of a bricklayer. Photograph by author.

movie *Przygoda na Marienstzacie* and the painting *Podaj cegłę* feature the brick as a symbol of Stakhanovite toil (Ibid).

The Palace of Culture and Science, unquestionably the icon of Warsaw's skyline and the pinnacle of Social Realism in Poland, was a 'gift' from Stalin to the Polish people (Crowley 1997, 213). It was constructed between 1952 and 1955 using imported Soviet labourers and over 40 million bricks, also imported, that could have been used to alleviate the dire housing shortage. At a time when the government was trying to channel the patriotism of the Poles into support for the communist cause, this clear imposition from an external regime caused dissent and dissatisfaction with the Party (Crowley 1997, 214).

Social Realism was short-lived, and the influence of Modernist styles and a need for efficiency prompted a shift from brick to concrete construction. The numbers are telling: in 1956, prefabricated panels were used for only 1.5% of construction, but by 1966, the proportion had skewed to only 9% traditional brick construction (Ciborowski 1964, 303). Following the general program of standardization and industrialization, the fabrication of building components was consolidated in large factories. By 1980, as many as 160 factories were producing large panels that were used in over 80% of residential construction (Szafer 1972, 12). The strict regulations imposed on construction necessarily provoked a reaction from architects and urban designers, especially in the 1980s in the global context of postmodernism. Pleas for a return to humanism, an alternative to monotony, and a revaluing of the architectural profession resounded from groups such as 'Dom i Miasto,' which "interpreted postmodernism as the return of architecture to its roots, as the reclamation of architecture's language [...]" (Królikowski 2012, 32).

Brick began to reenter the language of architecture, this time purposefully left exposed as a protest against large-scale prefabrication and the restrictions of Socialist Modernism. Its power as a human-scaled material, as well as its archaic connotations, made it the ideal medium for postmodernist thought. The church of Our Lady of Czestochowa exemplifies these concerns, with an added note of irony due to its location right next to the Trasa Łazienkowska highway. The Trasa Łazienkowska was constructed in the 1970s and clearly embodies Modernist ideals of monumentality and construction for the scale and speed of the car. In contrast, the forms of the church are fragmented, referencing a medieval cloister, and the buildings of the complex are entirely wrapped in modulating shades of yellow and red brick. The deeply recessed mortar joints of the highway side facade emphasize the individuality of each unit. Bricks are even turned on their ends and used as brise-soleil in front of the windows, further drawing attention to their uniqueness. Describing the drawings of the project executed by Tomasz Turczynowicz, the church's main architect, Jeremi Królikowski writes:

> The architecture of socialist modernism showed contempt for man while, regardless of the influence of postmodernist ideas, the architectural drawing of Tomasz Turczynowicz results from the aesthetics of sympathy. Stroke by stroke, brick by brick, every detail and element- all these find their individuality and selfhood in architecture that is alive and directly speaks to a man (Królikowski 2012, 32).

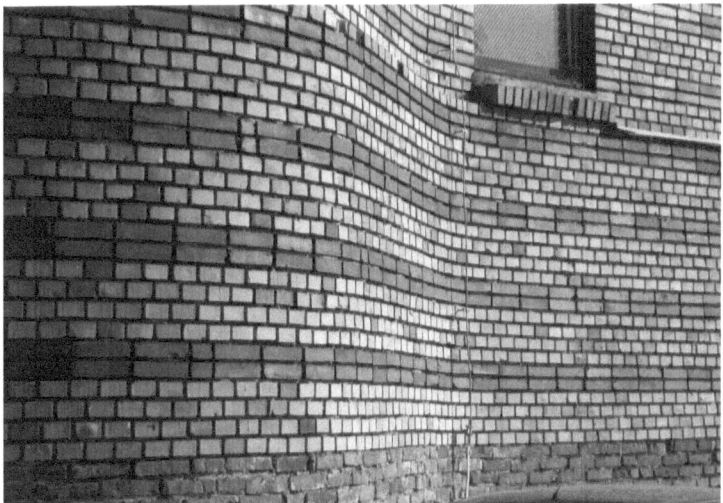

Detail of The church of Our Lady of Czestochowa. Photograph by author.

Prestige and Potential

Many of the criticisms of Socialist Modernism – monotony, lack of place-specificity, ignorance of the human scale – could also be applied to the ubiquitous curtain-walled condominiums and office towers prevalent in urban settings today, of which Warsaw has its fair share. Interestingly, clay also plays a dominant role in modern Polish construction in the form of insulating blocks that act as infill for

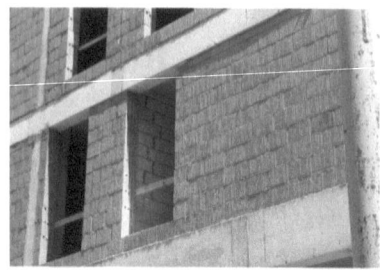

New walls made of clay block. Photograph by author.

a concrete frame; however, these blocks are always covered with perimeter insulation and cladding or render.

Brick's "capability to demonstrate prestige" (Roguska 2009, 33) is obviously still thought of as minimal. Prestige is a top priority for Warsaw, a city seeking to repress its past and affirm its place in Europe and beyond. This has resulted in the creation of projects such as the new National Stadium, built on the site of the 10 Year Anniversary stadium constructed in 1955 using rubble from the downtown, and the Złota 44 apartment tower, only a block away from the last remaining fragment of the ghetto wall and marketed as "the highest purely residential tower in the European Union."[10] These new architectures privilege the image over the texture, the skyline over the groundline, the eternal present over the palimpsest of history. Perhaps it is time for another revolution, one in which the generic metropolis is replaced with site-specific, material-based forms of urbanism.

With its shapes, textures, and assemblies, brick has the potential to acknowledge the incredible potency of Warsaw's history and also its potential for the future: a future which does not rely on the concept of tabula rasa or the propagation of globally recognizable images but thrives on the complexities and contradictions of a specific place. Unlike the superficiality of applied images, brick carries meaning within its substance. It is a source of both form and information. It constructs the city, and holds the city's memories.

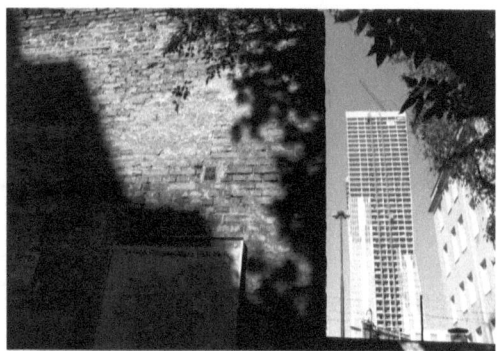

The Jewish Ghetto Wall with the Złota 44 apartment tower in the background. Photograph by author.

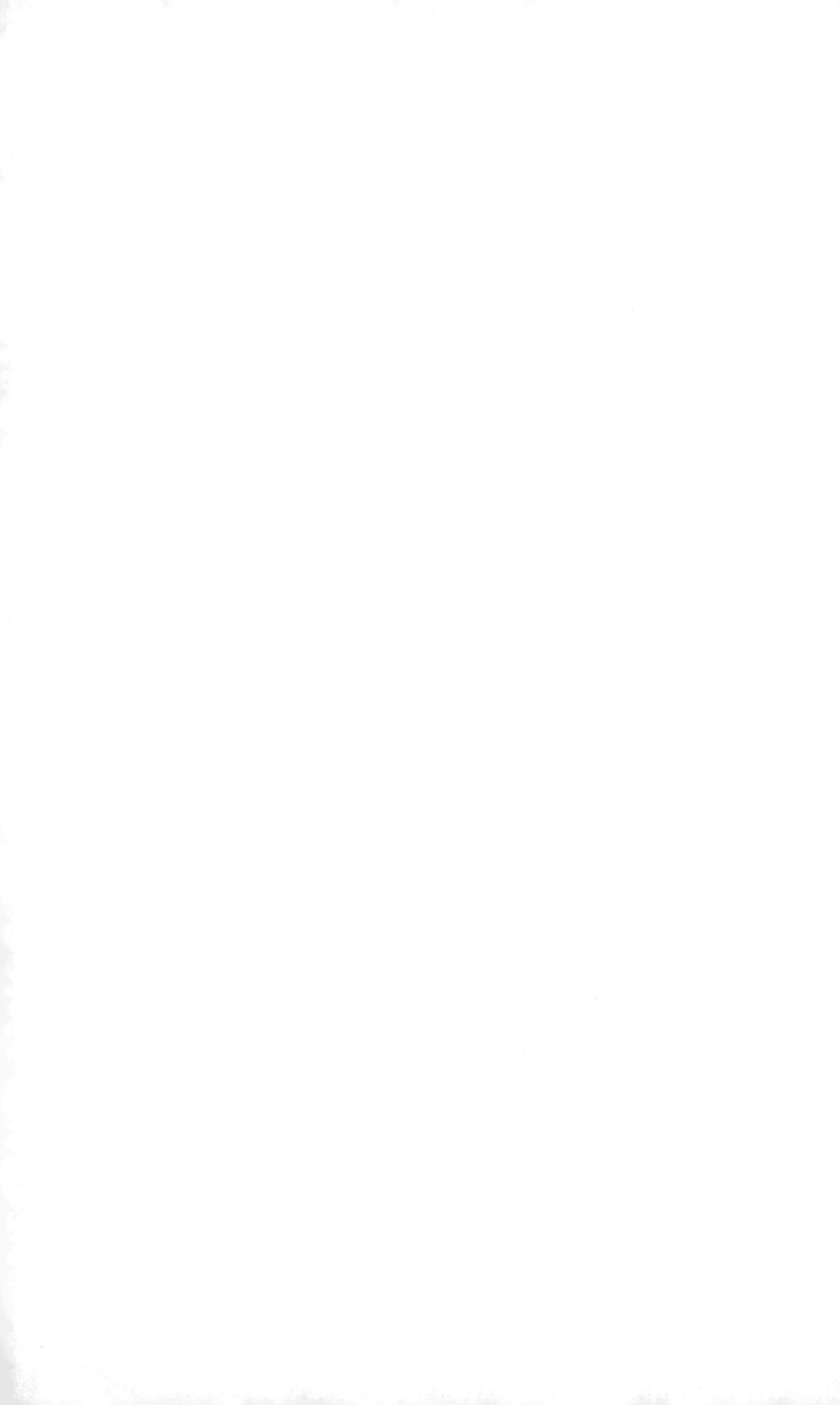

Saint-Henri and the Urban Uncanny

Emma Kreiner

Saint-Henri and the Urban Uncanny

Emma Kreiner

> *But even if life is tough, and the weather is harsh*
> *Even if we're hungry and we're cold and we're out of work*
> *Even on those long endless days on welfare, dragging our feet, we don't worry*
> *So hats off! Cause we can still laugh in Saint-Henri.*
> - Raymond Levesque, "À Saint-Henri" (theme song to Hubert Aquin's *À Saint Henri le cinq septembre*, 1962)

Hubert Aquin's *À Saint Henri le cinq septembre* (1962), and Shannon Walsh's *Saint-Henri The 26th of August* (2011) are documentary two films that were produced by the National Film Board of Canada (NFB), a governmentally affiliated film producer and distributor established in 1939. The two films depict a neighbourhood of Montréal that was once a suburban frontier of Canadian industry.[11] The documentaries, which I will refer to succinctly as *le cinq septembre* and *The 26th of August*, were made in and about the the post-industrial and rapidly gentrifying neighbourhood of Saint-Henri on late-summer days, bookending almost half a century. By way of introduction, I discuss the socio-historical and economic beginnings of Saint-Henri, and its development from a thriving industrial community into a gentrifying and divided post-industrial space. I then provide descriptions of these films that, beyond simply portraying a community, create a psychogeographic landscape.[12] In their entirety, Walsh and Aquin's films can be seen as small fragments of the temporal whole of Saint-Henri, and as pieces that fit together to form a montage of community. Ultimately, this paper examines how socio-historical realities of Saint-Henri were depicted in Aquin and Walsh's films, and will intend to demonstrate how an in-depth analysis of these films will uncover the causes and effects of shifting, uncanny perceptions of space and the positions of people within it.

A neighbourhood in constant threat, both recent and historic records of Saint-Henri have been underwritten with tones of urgency and danger. While themes of poverty, decay, re-development, and uncertainty are revealed in Aquin and Walsh's films, these pressing issues are left unresolved as the screens fade to black. Yet, site-seeing, or the filmic viewing of Saint-Henri, situated in the shadow of downtown Montréal, has the potential to facilitate a productive re-activation – one that, if not embodied, nonetheless impacts the viewer politically and emotionally.

A Post-Industrial Palimpsest

Although industry was quickly established in Saint-Henri, the infrastructure needed to foster the construction of a social community was not. In his thesis,

"Industry and Space: The Making of Montreal's Industrial Geography 1850-1918," Robert David Lewis explained that Saint-Henri was hindered by a "massive program of tax exemptions for industry which was harnessed to a policy of minimal provision of basic infrastructures and control over the working-class habitat" (Lewis 1992, 428). Subsequently, while Saint-Henri was a profitable industrial area up until the mid-1900s, it lacked a community-based identity. The neighbourhood was appealing to industrial firms because of its ideal transportation connections to the rest of Montreal and its easily accessible and cheap labour force. Saint-Henri's distinguishing factor, however, was the availability and malleability of space (Ibid, 461). As Lewis further contended, "Saint-Henri, in contrast to middle-class suburbs such as Notre Dame de Grâce, Westmount and Outremont, established a set of municipal policies which favoured business interests over those of their residents" (Ibid, 349). Therefore, when factories began to close in the late 1950s and the Fordist model of capitalism waned and collapsed, the inhabitants of Saint-Henri were faced with a disadvantage that was two-fold. The failure of industry left the citizens of Saint-Henri without satisfactory comfort or sufficient capital.

Neighbourhoods in Montreal are some of the most unequal and segregated in Canada, in terms of income (Gauthier, Jaeger, and Prince 2009). Of these, Saint-Henri is an example of the 'other half' of Canadian society, and was at one point listed amongst the worst inner-city slums in North America (Lewis 1992, 351). Once the epicentre of Canadian industry, thick with refineries, mills and factories, Saint-Henri was prosaically referred to as 'Smokey Valley' because of the ubiquity of manufacturing in the area.

A serious recession in Quebec between 1957 and 1961 culminated in an elevated unemployment rate in the province, which exceeded 14% during the winter of 1960. Correspondingly, between 1956 and 1961, the population of Saint-Henri decreased at a rate of 9.6% (O'Loughlin et al 1999, 1891). The economic crisis occurring during this period, along with a larger cultural, social, and political shift, was paralleled by the transformation from a rural and folk society to a modern and urban one. It can be argued that modern Quebec was born June 22, 1960, with Jean Lesage's election as premier. Lesage's policies were at the heart of the Quiet Revolution, in which language and the ethos of nationalism were central themes. At this moment, there was a need to stimulate the Quebecois art scene, and in 1961 the provincial government funded the Office du film du Quebec, that, together with the French division of the National Film Board, led to the production of many Quebecoise films. According to Fernand Dumont, a Quebecois sociologist, philosopher, and poet, "The Quiet Revolution seemed to be a cultural revolution, not only involving intellectuals, writers and artists, but occurring as well in the new mass media of film and television" (Lortie 2004, 45). The National Film Board was instrumental in this transformation. However, despite the emergence of this new Quebec cinema, that developed the themes of the Quiet Revolution and took a critical look at society, the inequalities they sought to expose only became more pronounced, and poverty did not go away (Ibid, 50).

In the 1960s, around the time Aquin completed his study of Saint-Henri, there were massive changes in the way cities were being structured, thought about, and depicted. In his book *Postmetropolis*, Edward Soja cited a change that was being initiated during the 1960s that can be described as a 'crisis-generated restructuring process.' Likewise, Pierre Gravel also described the massive transformations that occurred in Montreal during this period in his 1969 book *À Perte Des Temps*:

> Concrete, glass and steel girders. Twenty, thirty, fifty stories high. To tell the truth, the city didn't exist. In its place, a big, huge, monstrous thing that had never been given a name sprawled around a mountain and ended by dwindling into suburbs: east, west, north, a few scattered slums…In the centre, glass and girders. An artificial heart… it's was hard to talk about it as a city. And in fact, people didn't talk about it: they lived in it (Gravel 1969, 26).

Almost half a century later Saint-Henri was a predominantly Francophone neighbourhood of 25,000 people (less than half of the district's population in 1961) and was one of the most disadvantaged urban communities in Canada (O'Louglin et al 1999, 1891). A mixture of public housing projects and private speculation, in contemporary Saint-Henri, in contrast to its earlier iterations, economic emphasis is placed on real-estate development. The totality of this shift has marred the visual heritage of the neighbourhood, cutting off links to the past through the demolition of buildings, and limiting the expressions of individuality through the construction of condominiums that vary only slightly from each other.

Documenting Saint-Henri

The central subject of Hubert Aquin's 1962 film was not the people portrayed in *À Saint Henri le cinq septembre*, but the neighbourhood of Saint-Henri itself. In a travelogue fashion, Aquin brought the background into the foreground, and made the setting more important than the characters that traversed through it. With twelve camera-operators, Aquin was able to establish an all-seeing perspective that he complimented with sombre tones of an omniscient narrator. Shot in black and white and set to a soundtrack of melancholy accordion, portraits of the inhabitants of Saint-Henri were expertly framed, seamlessly edited together, and narrated over so that they converged to create a patchwork quilt of community. Aquin's film began with the sun rising over smoky rail yards, with a kind of quiet that is particular to early morning. The observer is immediately taken on a tour of Saint-Henri from the back of a milk bottle delivery truck, which zoomed through narrow streets with abandon and situates the viewer in the crowded south-western corner of Montreal. Aquin's narrator mentioned that this day was not chosen at random, but was the very important first day of a new school year. From the early morning to late into the night, Aquin documented this day with extreme attention to detail and with apodictic certainty. No single character dominates *le cinq septembre*, but images of energetic children, ambling teenagers, and seemingly stagnant adults move across the screen rapidly, so that the observer does not get a chance to really 'get to know' any of the characters. Aquin's shots are short in the English version of his film. In contrast, in the French version, a few characters, such as an unemployed labourer, are allotted ample time to speak about their hardships, or to simply be observed. Moments such as these become painful scenes of enforced stillness. Families, individuals, and small groups on the streets of Saint-Henri were depicted in their homes, in barbershops, restaurants, bars, nightclubs, police stations, and schools.

The film was composed in the cinema verité format, defined by Hubert Smith as a style that "gets as close as possible to the visual, aural, and kinaesthetic sense of actual presence. And it is a [style] that while compressing, re-arranging, and juxtaposing the bits and pieces of reality, adheres to the truth of the story" (Smith 1967, 58). Hubert Aquin's separatist leanings are not made explicit in his depiction of Saint-Henri, instead, the film's revelatory qualities lend to its revolutionary attributes. Specifically, the film's straight, factual style and omnipresent narration create an undercurrent of authority and truthfulness, that then enabled Aquin to collapse his political conceptions with images of the hard-working yet ill-fated residents of Saint-Henri. In *Writing Quebec*, Aquin's opinions are made clear. He pronounced, "the psychological implications caused by the awareness of the minority position [include]: self-punishment, masochism, a sense of unworthiness, 'depression' [...] and cultural fatigue" (Aquin 1988, 35). Aquin went on to state, "French Canada is a dying, tired culture" (Ibid, 44). This sentiment is manifested in *le cinq septembre*, as stagnancy and unemployment are caught in images of forcibly stilled middle-age men, while the film opens with men shouldering the weight of a coffin (**Fig. 1**) and closes with the threat of late-night danger.

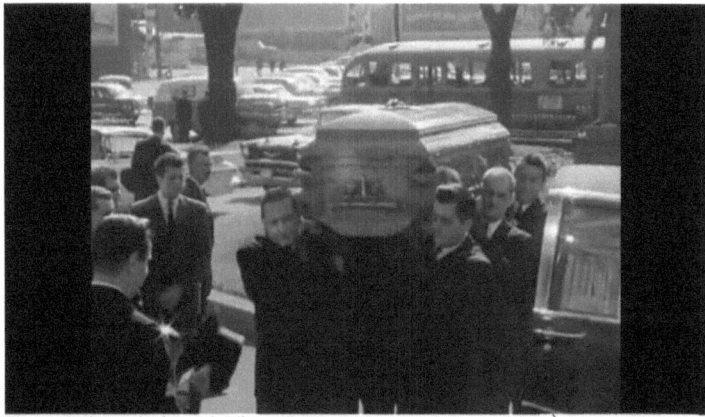

Figure 1. An early funeral. Film still (07:09) from Hubert Aquin's *À Saint Henri le cinq septembre* (1962) Dist.: NFB.

Aquin's depiction reflects the collective feeling of discontent and mobilization in the 1960s. As stated by André Lortie, at this moment in Quebec,

> Union leaders, intellectuals, and militants all sought to establish links with social movements. The deterioration in housing conditions, the absence of low-cost housing, and the inadequacy of social services fuelled the discontent that mobilized residents of disadvantaged neighbourhoods and spurred the creation of citizen action groups. Young people with degrees in the social sciences read Marx, discovered the 'culture of poverty,' moved into

neighbourhoods like Pointe Saint-Charles and Saint-Henri, and became social activists (Lortie 2004, 41).

Lortie forgot to mention that they also made documentaries about these neighbourhoods.

Authority is a constant theme in *le cinq septembre*, wherein sombre images of policemen loading their guns were juxtaposed with jovial portraits of young people socializing. In her book on the NFB, Zoë Druick explained that many NFB films are made with a pedagogical purpose, and show people in institutionalized settings (Druick 2007, 26). However, *le cinq septembre* Aquin critiqued the institutions that patronized Quebecois people, namely the government. This is overtly communicated in a scene in which young men sit in a bar and are shown laughing emphatically, perhaps one of the most light-hearted scenes of the film (**Fig. 2**). The narrator then reveals that the men were laughing about the mayor of Montreal.

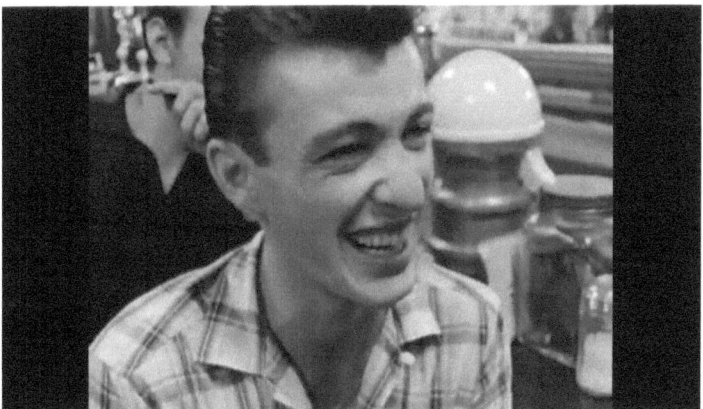

Figure 2. Sharing a laugh at the mayor's expense. Film still (22:36) from Hubert Aquin's *À Saint Henri le cinq septembre (1962)* Dist.: NFB.

In *le cinq semptembre*, well-groomed students in black and white uniforms, knee socks, and tunics stand in perfect order below the school's principal who delivers an obligatory welcome lecture. Children are very important in Aquin's film, for they serve to represent both the people of Saint-Henri, their fragility, strength, and hope for the future (**Fig. 3**). The young students are anxious as their strict principal delivers his first lecture of the year. Their eyes dart around the schoolyard with anxiety, curiosity, and boredom. A feeling of impending doom is present throughout.

As night fell, a fight broke out, and bloodied, drunken men were thrown into the back of a police car. As a young man sat in a barbershop chair getting a shave, an uneasy feeling hovers that the razor may slip at any moment. The honking of trains, factory whistles, and police sirens typified the mundane struggle of life, while funerary bells annotated its ending. Danger and death were largely unseen but always felt.

Aquin painted the banalities of this September day with subtle strokes of anger. At this point, however, it should be mentioned that Hubert Aquin himself was not a resident of Saint-Henri. In the 1960s, Aquin lived in the francophone intellectual quarter of Montréal, a square kilometre within the Plateau-Mont Royal, and was an outsider to the trivialities and impoverished circumstances that

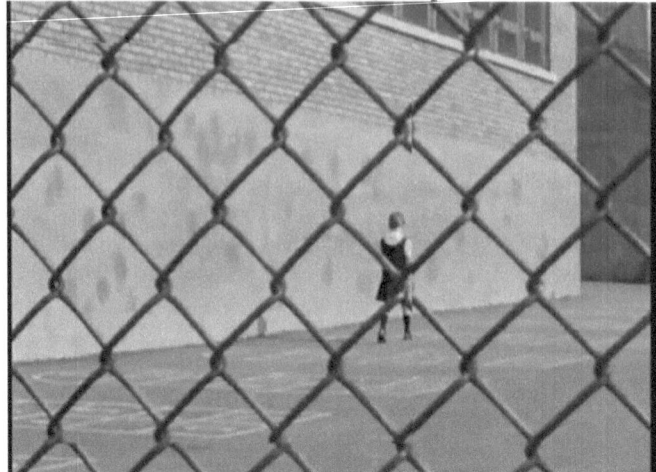

Figure 3. A study in isolation. Film still (05:10) from Hubert Aquin's *À Saint Henri le cinq septembre* (1962) Dist.: NFB.

he was representing. Nonetheless, Aquin believed language to be the most effective tool of action in the effort to reverse the psychological implications caused by the awareness of a minority position, which he considered to be the position of all French Canadians. For him, the artist was a 'professional of unhappiness' – he saw unhappiness as a sign of deep commitment, of protest, involving a greater level of consciousness (Aquin 1988, 4). Perhaps this is why Aquin's *le cinq Septembre* is so melancholic, and portrays a relatively mute majority, silenced by heavy-handed narration. The superimposed voice hovering over every action in Aquin's Saint-Henri creates the feeling that what is being shown is on the brink of disappearance and must be memorialized.

Aquin saw Saint-Henri, and Quebec as a whole, as having experienced cultural fatigue, retained in "a collective unconscious, the product of two centuries of repressed desire" (Ibid, xiii). Consequently, he intended to illustrate this to the rest of the country. Authority is a constant theme in *le cinq septembre*, wherein sombre images of policemen loading their guns are juxtaposed with jovial portraits of young people socializing. Glaring reminders of human powerlessness and impending death haunt the film throughout.

Inspired by Aquin's film but not beholden to it, Shannon Walsh's documentary is an homage that stands on its own. In 2011, Walsh conveyed an image of a Saint-Henri that had changed a great deal in fifty years since the making of Aquin's portrait in 1962. And while *The 26th of August* is structured around the shadowing of characters, the shadows in Walsh's film appear to be literally erased. The film is so overexposed that the whites are blown out and the detail in the darks is not detectable. The heightened brightness of the picture makes Saint-Henri appear as if it was a fantasy, and with this device, Walsh transforms a rough landscape into a whimsical post-industrial playground.

Doris is an articulate gleaner who led the camera along the streets and back alleys of Saint-Henri, and perhaps the most informative character in Walsh's film (**Fig. 4**). Doris is both a tour guide of the neighbourhood and a symbol for Saint-Henri itself. She spoke to the camera with certainty and declared, "Saint-Henri was not like it was." Doris explained, "We are all on welfare…In Saint-Henri there is no middle class. You're either rich or poor, there is no in-between."[13] She goes on to share her memories of a Saint-Henri of the past, when the factories were open and the young people had faith. Yet by 2011, the era of industrial wealth and collectivist culture in Saint-Henri had passed. Old and dilapidated, yet having to adapt to incursion and redevelopment, like *The 26th of August*, Doris clung to nostalgia while expressing hope for an improved future. Her hair is two-toned, with a grey stripe emerging from the centre of her skull, while dark red dye clings to the rest of her frail mane. Her teeth seem to hang delicately in her mouth, while her skin has been turned leathery by the sun.

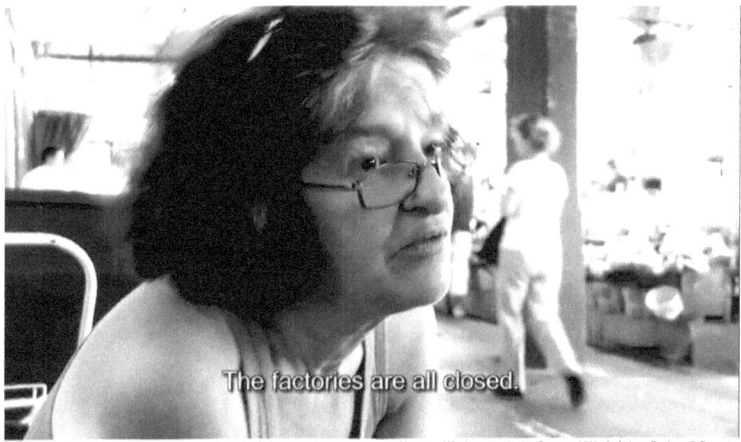

Figure 4. <u>One of Doris' many pithy statements</u>. Film still (1:00:30) from Walsh's *Saint-Henri the 26th of August*. (2011) Dist.: NFB & Parabola Films.

As she rummaged through discarded fruits and vegetables at the Atwater Market, in the background a voice on the radio spoke prophetically, and said: "In fact, there is a problem with time. We don't really want time to pass us by, but we delude ourselves into thinking it does. And that's the lie we tell ourselves. Time doesn't pass at all. We do. Time is what stays." Perhaps by choosing to depict dilapidated buildings and geriatric characters, Walsh was attempting to communicate the fragility of physical in urban spaces. By 2011, much of Saint-Henri stood in elegant dilapidation and could appear to an outsider as nothing more than an industrial wasteland.

Although Saint-Henri has been a neighbourhood historically oriented towards industry, it has been gentrified today. This gentrification is illustrated in Walsh's trailing of Doris, who seems disoriented by her environment. She leads the camera out to the front of a large apartment building, and calls up at an unnamed balcony-dweller, "Does Charles still live here?" The man addressed undoubtedly has no idea who Charles is and turns Doris away (**Fig. 5**). This sequence illustrates that Saint-Henri is a home in which its inhabitants are constantly having to re-orient themselves towards an ever-shifting, uncanny space.

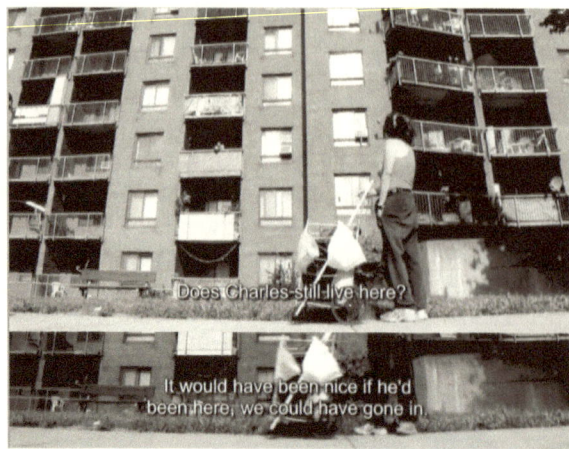

Figure 5. Doris' uncanny spatial experience. Film still (21:07) of Walsh's *Saint-Henri the 26th of August.* (2011) Dist.: NFB & Parabola Films.

Deconstructing the Uncanny in Saint-Henri

From the German *heimlich*, which mutates into the unheimlich, translated into English as the homely and unhomely, 'the uncanny' is rooted in the conversion of an object, place, or person that was once familiar into something decidedly not. In his 1919 essay "The Uncanny," founder of psychoanalysis Sigmund Freud attempted to pin down the multiple etymologies and meanings of the uncanny, that he primarily identifies as being based on a theory of feeling rather than one of aesthetics. Borrowing from Freud, I proceed to discuss the uncanny in Saint-Henri in two segments: the first is concerned with the alienation engendered when subjects are confronted with a reflection of themselves, and the second is an analysis of the architectural and interruptive re-generation of Saint-Henri, transforming it from a familiar to an unfamiliar space.

As Walter Benjamin argued, urban meanings are not only bound up in physical forms of the city. For him, these forms gave themselves to the subject at different moments and a sense of material space was filtered through experience (Tonkiss 2005, 120). Or in simpler terms, a neighbourhood was defined to people by their experiences of it. Likewise, urban planners borrow the term 'cognitive mapping' from psychology, to describe how people make their way around the city (Ibid). Subsequently, in this investigation, 'cognitive mapping' is applied in a filmic sense. Film theorist Tom Conley argued, "A film can be understood in a broad sense to be a 'map' that plots and colonizes the imagination and the public it is said to 'invent' and as a result, seek to control" (Conley 2007, 1). In a sense then, the 'mapping' of space in film does more than simply reflect places, but it creates and re-creates them, often with an uncanny effect.

The shifting nature of both public and private spaces in Saint-Henri, as well as the translation of the neighbourhood and its inhabitants into a two-dimensional form, lends to a constant uncanny reality in Saint-Henri. However, rebellions against this pervasive alienation occur in the space of the city itself – *not* in film – a medium capable of only instantiating and disseminating the fragments of the urban experience. As spatial theorist Henri Lefebvre has declared, "Physical space has no 'reality' without the energy deployed within it" (Lefebvre 1991, 13). There is another reality, however, one in which creative and psychological processes reign supreme. Aquin and Walsh's brief screenings of the palimpsest that is Saint-Henri help to create a platform of knowledge and provide rich material from which to enter a dialogue of neighbourhood, thick with a multitude of tensions, values, and uses.

For the film theorist Guiliana Bruno, the uncanny exists in postmodern junk-space (**Fig. 6**). Bruno states, "the effects of the postmodern, industrial condition are: wearing out, and waste" (Bruno 1987, 64).

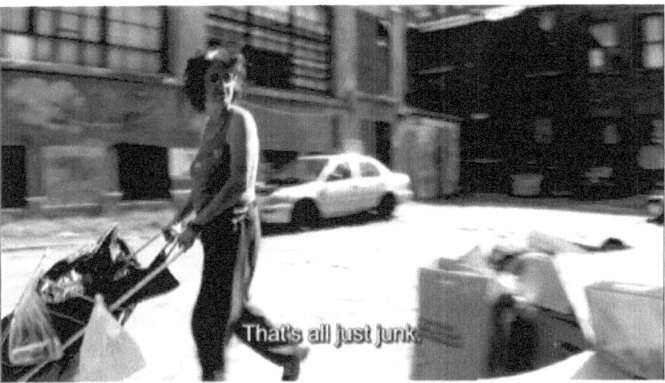

Figure 6. Doris gleaning. Film still (5:17) from Walsh's *Saint-Henri the 26th of August*. (2011) Dist.: NFB & Parabola Films.

She outlines the aesthetics of the postmodern condition, as resulting from discontinuous signifiers, such as the unfettered construction of condos in Saint Henri, and erosion, such as the wearing away and removal of industrial and residential buildings in the community. Much of the physical space in Aquin's and Walsh's films can be looked at through Bruno's lens, and perhaps more so in Walsh's depiction of gentrification and decay. Evidence of this junk-space exists in Walsh's representation of the crumbling Turcot interchange (**Fig. 7**), which was set for reconstruction at the time *the 26th of August* was being made.

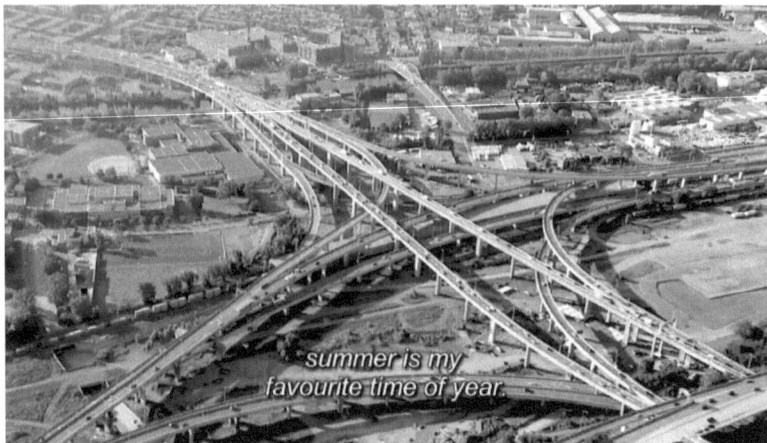

Figure 7. The Turcot Interchange. Film still (00:57) from Walsh's *Saint-Henri the 26th of August*. (2011) Dist.: NFB & Parabola Films.

The City's plan for reconstruction would have required the demolition of a significant portion of the Village des Tanneries neighbourhood on the western edge of Saint-Henri, causing much controversy and inching Saint-Henri closer to the uncanny. Another example of demolition and uncanny architectural spaces depicted in Walsh's film are the Canada Malt Silos (**Fig. 8**).

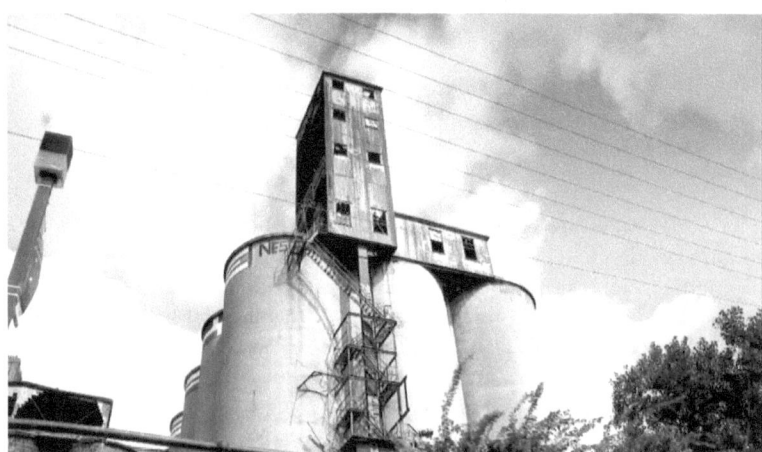

Figure 8. The Canada Malt Silos. Film still (1:01:50) from Walsh's *Saint-Henri the 26th of August*. (2011) Dist.: NFB & Parabola Films.

The silos are an architectural sight distinctive and elemental to the skyline of Saint-Henri. Tattooed with graffiti, squatted in, and climbed up, a rusty cylindrical structure simultaneously real and imagined, the Silos are intrinsic to the collective imagination of the community. However, despite their historical place and imaginative possibilities, the Silos are now set be torn down and replaced with condominiums. In Saint-Henri, once-cheap rents are rising, and the social mix of the neighbourhood is drastically changing.

The uncanny does not *only* hover over the continuing physical transformation of Saint-Henri, but it also is inherent in the medium of film used to document it, that transfers lived-reality into a two-dimensional image, literally creating a double. However, this double reality is also evident in the city itself. Likewise, three-quarters of a century after Freud termed the uncanny, the architectural historian Anthony Vidler further developed this concept: "The uncanny as articulated by Freud is rooted in the domestic environment. It opens up problems of the self, the other, the body and its absence, relations between psyche and dwelling, the body and the house, the individual and the metropolis" (Vidler 1992, x). In the Saint-Henri films, we are rarely shown images of architectural interiors, though the ones we do see are closet-like (**Fig. 9**).

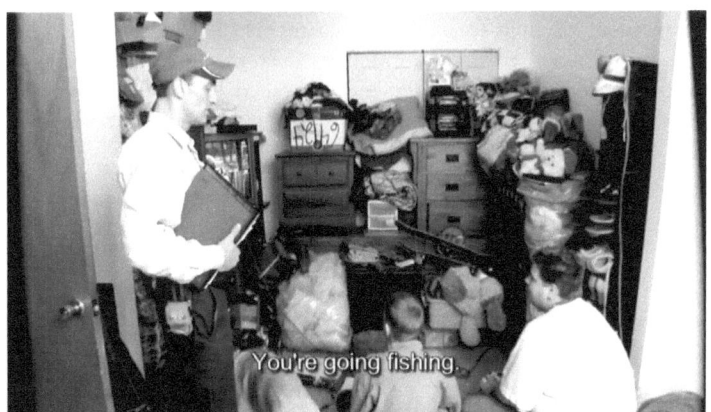

Figure 9. A Saint-Henri interior. Film still (12:33) from Walsh's *Saint-Henri the 26th of August*. (2011) Dist.: NFB & Parabola Films.

Instead of interiors, we are privy to images of people congregating on thresholds that seem to symbolize the connection that inhabitants of Saint-Henri have with their exterior environment. However, the type of habitation depicted in both documentaries appears too simplified. In both films, a problematic revelry exists in the austerity of living in Saint-Henri. Aquin's vision seems to be in-line with this hypothesis, as his film attempted to depict people made authentic through their impoverished circumstances. To illustrate this point, one of Aquin's cinematographers, Fernand Dansereau, wrote that the response to *le cinq septembre* was "astonishingly violent." He stated, "[The people of Saint Henri] felt debased by our outsiders' observations of them. Worse yet, certain people who played a role in the film felt deeply and personally hurt. One of the families that had been filmed, for example, was overcome with a sort of shame so strong that they decided to remove their children from the local school" (Mackenzie 1997, 72). As Edward Soja has pronounced,

> The city exists as a series of doubles; it has official and hidden cultures, it is a real place and a site of imagination. Its elaborate network of streets, housing, public buildings, transport systems, parks and shops is paralleled by a complex of attitudes, habits, customs, expectations and hopes that reside in

us as urban subjects. We discover that urban 'reality' is not single but multiple, that inside the city there is always another city (Soja 2000, 324).

Hence, in creating a fixed image of Saint-Henri, Aquin removed the opportunity for the multiple realities that constantly emerge and are redefined.

In his book *The Architecture of the Uncanny*, Anthony Vidler offered, "The Uncanny can be found in the transformation of something that once seemed homely into something decidedly not," (Vidler 1992, 6) and went on to elucidate that the uncanny erupts in "the wasted margins and surface appearances of post-industrial culture" (Ibid, 3). This is witnessed in Walsh's recent portrayal by the ubiquitous intrusion of condominium developments, which create a socio-spatial polarization between the affluent and the poor. Where in Saint-Henri there was once a precedent of built-for-the-poor tenements, a relatively recent trend of pervasive built-for-the rich condominiums has changed the feeling of the neighbourhood (**Fig 10**). One condo project, called *Bassins Du Havre*, located in Griffintown, just east of Saint-Henri, describes their condominium as if it were a lush oasis in the middle of wasteland.

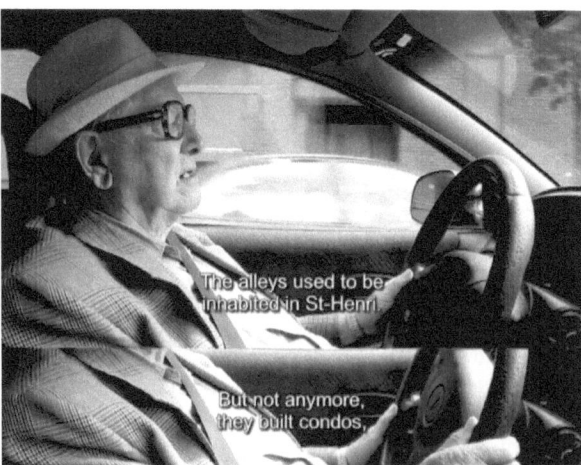

Figure 10. Robert commenting on architectural developments. Film still (9:30) from Walsh's *Saint-Henri the 26th of August.* (2011) Dist.: NFB & Parabola Films.

This company, among many others, markets dwellings to the well-compensated bourgeoisie, and creates what Michael Dear dubs 'commudities' – shorthand for commodified communities – created expressly to satisfy and profit from the bourgeoisie (Klingman 2007, 286). The *Bassins Du Havre* pamphlet states: "Outstretched buildings look like they've been carefully placed on the water. Back from your daily ride on the famous Lachine Canal bike path, stop for a moment and take in the fine architectural details reflected in the water. You're surrounded by a relaxed atmosphere and away from the concrete jungle…and yet, just minutes from downtown!" In these herculean buildings, one's experience with others is often not in the street, but in the elevator, if at all. This style of living corresponds with Jean Baudrillard's account of private 'telematics,' in which

Each person sees himself at the controls of a hypothetical machine, isolated in a position of perfect and remote sovereignty, at an infinite distance from his universe of origin. Which is to say, in the exact position of an astronaut in his capsule, in a state of weightlessness that necessitates a perpetual orbital flight and a speed sufficient to keep him from crashing back to his planet of origin (Baudrillard 1983, 128).

In this instance, Baudrillard's prophetic astronaut in capsule could be taken as a metaphor from which to consider the risk of missing the creative activity, symbolism, and play that exist on the level of the ground.

Described by Aquin as "a little island, surrounded by water, railroads, and the industrial wealth of other men," Saint-Henri has been subject to the kind of isolation that creates the conditions for internalized exile, but those which can also encourage forms of alternative engagement with space that rupture the rules for living that are expressed by governments, developers, and police forces. Henri Lefebvre has stated, "Spatial opposition can take place through staged encounters, explicit manoeuvres and sometimes through pitched battles, but also via little incursions into official territory, small acts of resistance" (Cited in Tonkiss 2005, 64). This is evident in both Aquin and Walsh's films, where we see people re-appropriating spaces, such as boys who use a bridge as their diving board (**Fig. 11**); a gleaner who searches through dumpsters for her daily wages; young people who appropriate abandoned spaces to fraternize and practice knife throwing; graffiti artists who use back-alleys as their galleries; a man who does his afternoon laps in the canal; and even a couple who climb up an abandoned factory to get a good view of the city. Lefebvre outlined for us, "Except when society is defined exclusively by consumption… there is an awareness that consideration of isolated acts does not exhaust daily life, and that we must attend to their context: the social relations within which they occur" (Lefebvre 1991, 2). In documenting these social relations, it can be assumed that NFB films also depicted a *refusal* of daily life that Lefebvre goes on to state, "can be either heroic or ascetic, or hedonistic and sensual, or revolutionary, or anarchistic – in other words, new-romantic, hence aesthetic" (Ibid, 1). Correspondingly, Walsh and Aquin's compositions protest against spatial and visual hegemony and create new kinds of aesthetic knowledge about Saint-Henri, therefore interrupting the perception of the everyday. In his *Report on Post Modern Knowledge*, Jean-François Lyotard explained, "A remedy (for alienation and malaise) can come from changing the status of aesthetic experience when it is used to explore a living historical situation, that is, when it is put in relation with problems of existence" (Lyotard 1989, 71). Exploring a "living historical situation," and "changing the status of the aesthetic experience" of Saint-Henri are driving concerns of both Aquin and Walsh's films, although whether or not their works are successful in the endeavour to alleviate alienation is certainly subject to debate.

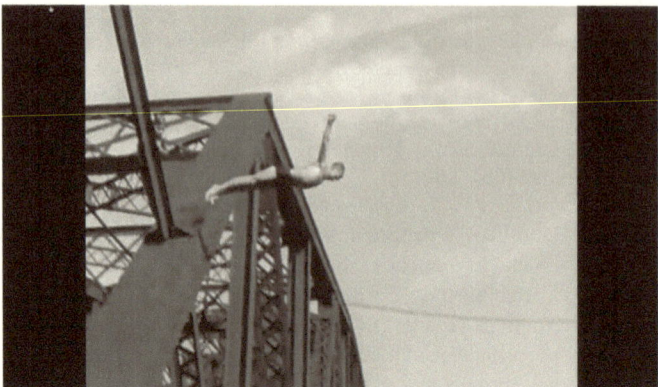

Figure 11. <u>Boy dives off bridge</u>. Film still (16:08) from Hubert Aquin's *A Saint Henri le cinq septembre* (1962) Dist.: NFB.

Perhaps we can take both Aquin and Walsh's films as small acts of resistance, as efforts to make changing surroundings somehow better understood. Similarly, this paper engenders dialogue about the connection between the provocative mediatized visualization of Saint-Henri, the conditions of everyday life in this neighbourhood, and questions of the emotional, physical, and psychological experiences of Saint-Henri, a community that seems to be in an extended moment of danger.

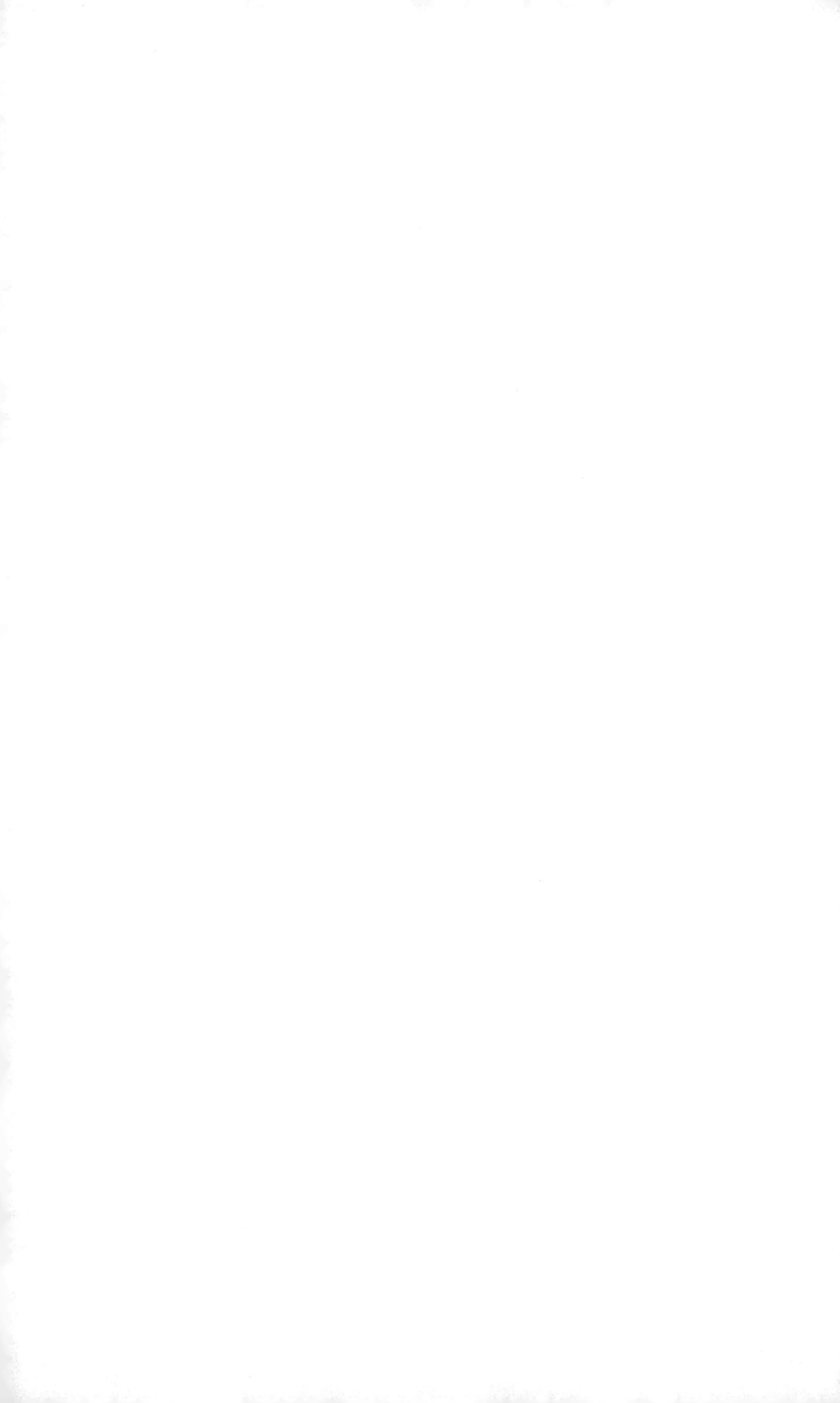

Kaitlynn McQueston

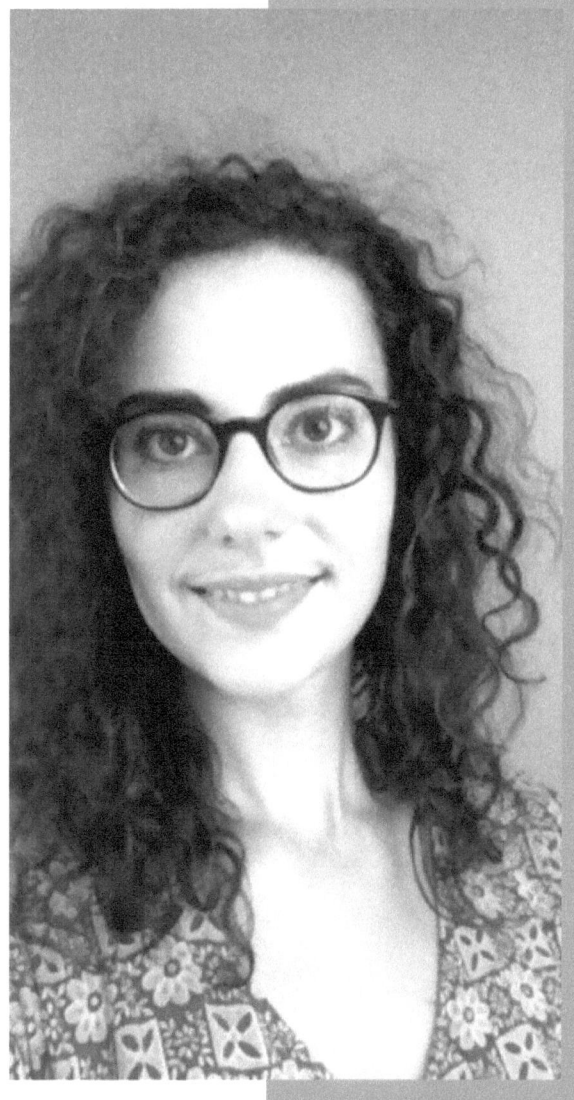

Pornaganda and the Felt Machine

Kaitlynn McQueston

Having parents who are labourers during the Mayoral term of Rob Ford is not easy. To say the least, being immersed in this anti-union, anti-labourer contemporary climate is not easy. Growing up, I had the luxury of seeing the nuances of Canadian labour politics through a very personal and immediate lens. In my experience, there is a subtle disconnect that some young people (without connections to labour) have with the world around them. This goes beyond the issues of workers' rights or class struggles, to include a lack of agency over the objects and materials in their lives.

I do concede to having perhaps an over-empathetic relationship with the workers of the industrial material world. Nevertheless, my naïve compassion has made me sensitive to the capricious nature of public opinion among youth. Advertisements and popular media have long been tools used to sway public opinion. Although the news in Toronto and Southern Ontario has become increasingly anti-labour, it is only in combination with physical reality that these voices have any staying power. As such, the reality that supports the media's anti-labour values is made physical in consumer objects.[14] Consumer objects as well as the objects in my art practice themselves are current forms of communication: a phenomenon that I call 3D Propaganda. Their transformation into social ideas and self-perpetuating desires has allowed them to function today as the propaganda itself. I argue that the construction of the object as such —in combination with the modern media — holds as much power to persuade us emotionally and socio-politically as, for example, the posters of WW2 Propaganda.

Although all people are vulnerable to this propaganda, I would argue that only youths whose livelihoods *depend* on labour have an inherited (as opposed to learned) repudiation of these forces. In this paper, I will expand on two projects that have fuelled my research, as well as the motivation behind them. Through these projects, along with my personal experience, I endeavor to explain how one's socio-political makeup is a vehicle for sensual perception and vice-versa.

After the advent of the post-war industrial design period known as Mid-Century Modern, consumer objects began to place less emphasis on function, quality, and good craftsmanship.[15] Instead, consumer objects began to be designed aesthetically to convey 'domestic bliss.' This is a characteristic that many contemporary consumer objects still possess. Being a capitalist society, a large portion of our economic health depends upon frivolous and impulsive consumer spending. A culture of labour and appreciation for the manufacturer must remain as separate as possible—for physical labour is neither frivolous nor impulsive. The values of the labouring world problematize the luxurious care-free and impulsive image that the consumer world tries to maintain. Perhaps it is for this reason that labour is never intentionally evident within the aesthetics of objects we purchase. Whether this is done purposefully, or as a reaction to the need to fill consumers with a desire for luxury— that they may or may not be able to afford— the act of hiding labour from the consumer has socio-political consequences in favor of those who wish to supress the labouring class. For this reason I refer to these objects as containing the 'ghost of labour' or an 'invisible labour.' When you see the making of the object, the process of production, or get close and examine the craft and strength of material, you encounter the ghost of labour. This functions like Walter Benjamin's aura of the artwork: objects command themselves to you the way words do (Benjamin 2008, 14). As such, our sociopolitical attitudes, I argue, can be studied through our relationship with industrial materials.

The ghost of labour is what allows the object's power to spill into the socio-political sphere. When the labour required to build an object is no longer a part of its being, the object transcends its physicality and becomes a vehicle for individual narcissistic desire (as opposed to a necessity) at the expense of the work of labourers. As it is, the objects deny the nature of themselves, including their own invention and history. In harmony with consumer objects, living a consumer lifestyle in a capitalist society is rooted in opposition to living a life as a labourer. Youth especially, being the target of most consumer ads, are vulnerable to these narcissistic anti-labour values via the popular commodities among them. Hence, the underlying classist nature of our society is easily awoken by media in combination with the underlying classism inherent in 3D Propaganda design, marketing and production.

3D Propaganda

I have always had strong feelings invested in the hands-on work of construction and maintenance, with my father being a mechanic and heavy equipment operator, and my mother being a gardener and landscaper. It is out of this personal history and experience with construction that I created *Engine*.

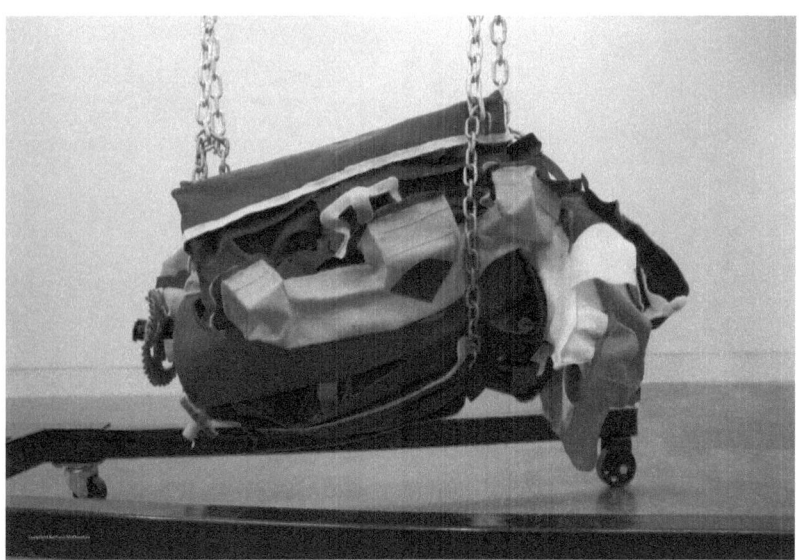

Kaitlynn McQueston, *Engine*, 2013, 3 ½ 'x 1 ½'x 1 ½', felt + hoist. Courtesy of the artist.

Engine (2013) is a to-scale V8 engine made entirely out of felt. It was assembled using only needle felting techniques. The fragile assembly of the machine in combination with its weight and awkward angles create openings in the sculpture that allow the viewer to peek into the body of the engine and see the parts. Although the engine is fully assembled and much of the mechanisms are encased and not visible, I allow the viewer to gently pull back the loose segments such as the cylinder caps, or use their hands to enter the soft engine and push layers out of the way to view very complex systems like the crankshaft or the oil pump.

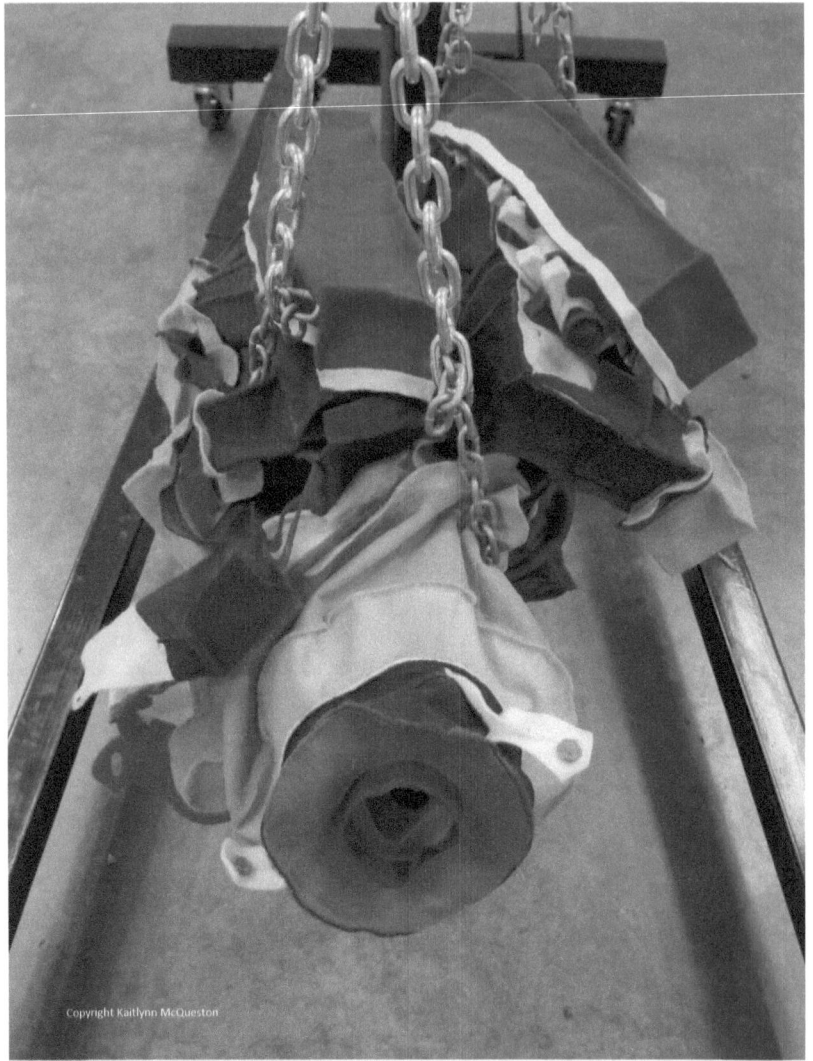

Kaitlynn McQueston, *Engine*, 2013, 3 ½ ’x 1 ½’x 1 ½’, felt + hoist. Courtesy of the artist.

The handcrafted nature of the piece allows one to approach a V8 engine in a drastically different way than one would the real thing. The welcoming nature of the fabric object, in combination with the non-threatening limpness of the intricate mechanical mechanisms, confronts the anxieties and excitement one experiences when faced with an object beyond one's understanding. My practice of working with materials and studying the ways objects communicate has led me to believe that hand-crafted objects allow, indeed often demand, an intimacy with the viewer due to their characteristic imperfections and expressiveness. This intimacy is absent in machine-made or machine-assisted objects produced for commercial consumption today, in which such idiosyncrasies are labeled as flaws and discarded. Mid-Century Modern discourse, discussed above, marked the resistance of these idiosyncrasies in industrial design. This aesthetic was pioneered not by the needs and interests of the public but by just a few leading scholars[16] of industrial design and was characterized by a very sleek geometric style governed by strict rules of mathematics.[17]

Fully enclosed casing and streamlined surfaces absent of flaw, adornment, or visible mechanisms were all distinctions belonging to the Mid-Century Modern aesthetic.[18] Many essential elements of this movement are found in consumer aesthetic because symmetrical form and simplicity of design is instrumental to the efficiency of mass production processes such as mould making and casting. This aesthetic has, consequentially, impacted our perception of which objects we deem suitable to perform for our needs. Furthermore, it has become the norm to conceal working mechanisms, depriving consumers of the chance to observe or engage with an object's inner construction. Given that good quality construction is often compromised in order to decrease labour costs, objects communicate their, often false, legitimacy through that which conceals their components: the outer surface.

For instance, compare a laptop or iPod to older tape players on which one could open the side to reveal the inner mechanisms. Much of this can be attributed to the complete digitization of things—there is no need for manual mechanical interfaces on an iPod other than the menu. The shift toward encasing and finishing objects has grown into an expectation. Moreover, this engineered norm can be related to the way the media has the power to engineer public opinions via object propaganda.[19] Objects have the potential to be much more manipulative than the media as they are not commonly conceived in this way. Our objects thus both create, and are created by, a society where it is commonplace to think of labour as unimportant.

In contrast to this dominant approach, *Engine* is meant to be inviting on a bodily level. It is soft fabric as opposed to steal; it is colourful, it is homemade, and yet it has all the working parts of a real automobile engine. I believe that seeing modern consumer objects as tools of propaganda allows for the opportunity to circumvent their manipulative forces.

Kaitlynn McQueston, *PORNAGANDA*, 2013, video work. Courtesy of the artist.

The above image is a still shot from a fifty-minute film (accessible at pornaganda.tumblr.com), wherein wood-grain slowly appears on human skin. To create this effect, I pressed my back against the wooden sidings of my house for approximately twenty minutes. When I moved away from the wall, the image of wood-grain remained on my skin as an impression and discolouration. I immediately stood in front of a video camera focused on my back and filmed my skin until the impression disappeared. I then reversed the video and played it in real time.

In the film, the body becomes a site for the beauty of industrial material textures. The texture is painted on my skin, has shaped my skin, and left its commanding mark. Previously, my house had only been a placeholder to support the roof before I did this work. Now, the material became a site for the human body to rest and a place for skin to touch.

We do not encounter the industrial material world in the same way that we encounter materials as consumer products. I initially did this experiment on a sidewalk where I had a similar experience. In opposition to domestic consumer design objects, industrial material — such as sidewalks and building exteriors — are sites of visible labour. Because they require constant maintenance, due to the public's reasonable expectations of quality (unlike consumer objects), we do not obscure their construction. Like language and images, industrial materials are important sites and mechanisms for cultural struggle. One such example of industrial materials that function as a site of cultural struggle is streets. As a case-in-point, streets are treated much differently in a general strike or protest started by labourers. A street demonstration is not just about using the sidewalk to move from A to B, it is about making the streets your own, feeling it as a home shared by all. With my art practice, then, perhaps reclaiming engagement and participation with the materials and working mechanisms of our objects has a power similar to that of reclaiming the streets.

Labour is not the only element of consumer objects that is hidden from the customer. The industrial materials are also ignored. The materials are only a means to an end and disappear seamlessly for the purpose of becoming consumable. In some cases, the less recognizable the material, the better. Without the presence of labour, consumer objects are no longer objects, they are ideas. These ideas — divorced from the object's function — are sold to us as abstract desires such as the desire to be popular, cool, or unique. Moreover, the creators of these objects, when the processes of creation are hidden, also become invisible.

Sexuality in Advertisements

Contemporary advertisements often employ sexuality as a hidden weapon of persuasion. In my *PORNAGANDA* project, the nature of persuasion is reversed. By putting sexuality at the forefront of the film discussed above, the film becomes a 'commercial' not for an object, but for the materials that produce the objects. Therefore, the traditional treatment of materials as merely a means to an end is refuted. I deny an object presence in the film. Only the ghost of a milled piece of wood from the side of my house presents itself, in the most intimate way, visible only by way of my body.

Engine functions in the opposite way. The piece shows the object without the material. The nature of felt fabric is ignored when it is manipulated to build something normally constructed of metal. Importantly, the material here does not merely serve function. Rather, I attempt to demonstrate how the materials influence how we perceive and interact with an object. In this way, I connect the consumer to the manufacture of the object, as opposed to the capitalist agenda where disconnecting the consumer from the manufacturer is essential. This is intended as a radical opposition to the idea that the state owns our material world and we do not. The idea that one cannot learn to make things, I believe, is a reaction to contemporary objects' denial of labour. Experiencing an object in a different material eradicates the immaculacy of the consumer object and allows the viewer to engage more fully with the inner construction of the machine.

I also situate this artwork within the "art vs. craft" debate. This debate concerns the consideration of crafts as less important than art because they are made to be bought and are more closely related to consumer items. Art, on the other hand, is perceived as more about creativity, ideas, and the beauty of life free from the cloud of profit. As a skilled worker, you learn to work in harmony with materials. It has been my goal to communicate that this is not an isolated, unimportant task guided by profit. Instead the engine is partially inspired by the unique folk culture among labourers which values socio-political wellbeing, hard work and materials as one; a characteristic some may attribute to an artist.

Concluding Remarks

Our sociopolitical makeup shapes our understanding of how things work. In my art practice, I seek to expose this interaction in reference to the labour industry and materials. *PORNAGANDA* and *ENGINE* address two complimentary processes: the engine is a symbol for industry, explaining the physical interactions with materials and the ways in which our material world has been socially constructed. In *PORNAGANDA*, I am physically close with the materials. I aim to understand my personal emotional attachment to not only the materials themselves, but also how the structures they compose came to be. This juxtaposition expresses the cultural transition constantly taking place between the material world and our desires.

The denial of labour necessitates that materials are obscured and instead seen only as their eventuality as objects. This denial has been imperative in the development of what I call Three-Dimensional Propaganda. 3D Propaganda relies on our unfamiliarity and lack of knowledge of the materials consumer goods are made from. It relies on removing the evidence of work from the object of consumption. It keeps manufacturing processes behind a seductive veil and works in the same way media propaganda surreptitiously uses sensory seduction to influence the masses. By neglecting the object in this way, one is subject to manipulation of the political psyche. Understanding mechanisms, feeling the ownership we rightfully have over the streets, and honouring the value of the materials our objects are made from are radical stands against the forces of propaganda that enforce a capitalist view of material objects and society as a whole. Pleasing the customer turns people into things. Instead, an appreciation of labour builds communities.

Ghosts of the Economic Image: Blanchot, Bataille, and the Non-Circulation of the Canadian Penny

Andew Kingston

Ghosts of the Economic Image: Blanchot, Bataille, and the Non-Circulation of the Canadian Penny

Andrew Kingston

The last Canadian penny entered into circulation at the end of February 2013, after which the Canadian government began the lengthy task of re-collecting these coins. The Canadian government set itself this task because the penny — the physical coin that represents one cent — actually cost Canada more than one cent to produce. As such, the government estimated that by eliminating the penny, it could save approximately eleven million dollars per year (Canada's Economic Action Plan). But beyond the productivity restored to the government by the spare change that it can save, how can the implications of such a dramatic change in currency be understood? Ultimately, at an economic level, this tactic has little to no effect on the functioning of late-capitalist marketplaces — the malfunctioning of which it is a result. Still, structurally speaking, what occurs here is quite literally a shift in the basis of economy, as the physical representative of the unit — literally the 'one' — of value, disappears. The disappearance of the cent, then, undermines the very basis for exchange, if only symbolically. Prices for non-cash purchases, for example, are unaffected by this change. Cash purchases, however, are rounded up or down to the closest power of five. Of course, this is little more than a shift of the basis of value from one to five. Yet inasmuch as non-cash transactions can still be accomplished at the level of the single cent, whereas cash transactions cannot, this opens up a sort of liminal space of exchange (or rather of non-exchange, non-exchangeability), lying at the heart of our cash-and-credit economies, making different forms of exchange non-exchangeable with each other. As this brief investigation will attempt to show, such a non-exchangeability reveals and undermines an imaginary economy, or economy of the image, upon which these different forms of exchange are predicated. The precariousness of this economy is what forces, in this case, the government of Canada to gather up and melt its coins as quickly as possible, rather than let them become a disruptive reflection of the arbitrary and restrictive system of value that it maintains.

The Image(s) of the Penny

To begin, one should first look at the face of the penny: it is an image, which already complicates the penny's status as an inert physical object. This image can be understood in two senses, which are ultimately linked. First, in the most obvious sense the image is of the face of an important living or deceased political figure—in this case: Queen Elizabeth II. As will be discussed in what follows, the image of the queen presents the face of a distant and ultimately irrecuperable lack of signification. However, what this coined portrait does on the surface is precisely the opposite — it recuperates a positive value from its engraving: a value of which an absent authority, the queen, is guarantor. In other words, the supplemented character of exchange value is already present in the coin's immediate representation. And yet, regardless of its supplement, the coin still maintains value: that of, in Marxian terms, the money-form. The unit and the unity of the exchangeability of commodities is reflected in the glint of even, and especially, the penny. This, then, is the first image that it presents: the immaterial and yet forceful effect of the system of commodity-exchange. In this sense, money in general is haunted by the presence of an immaterial force that possesses it while remaining outside of it, imbuing it with a value beyond its materiality. This is all basic. But here is found a first paradox, which has already in turn haunted the Canadian government: that the penny itself can for this reason cost more to make than it can hold within a supplementary economy of exchange value, of which it nonetheless remains the basis.

At the heart of this paradox is the fact that the penny presents an image that is not identical with itself, but already outside of itself, outside of its own control: the absent monarch, herald of another time and another world, anachronistically binds value to a set of rules that can no longer adequately function alongside its material basis. This is to say that the Canadian government and governments in general often derive their monetary figureheads from worlds that historically or fictionally prefigure their own, so as to hold their systems of representative value in check by linking them to a heritage that exceeds and overshadows fluctuations in their economy. The image of the queen, in this case, lies outside of the Canadian government's autonomy, and yet is maintained as a herald of Canada's identity, functioning, as Derrida would say, as a 'transcendental signified,' as the guarantor of the consistency of the signification of value. This ideological linkage that maintains the validity of the exchange value of money is paradoxically maintained by a bastardization, or recuperation of the fundamental force of its images: of the presence of an absence, a value that is simultaneously there and not there.

The Penny as Cadaver and as Ghost

The second sort of image to be found in the penny is contained in its immediate representation. This is first revealed by the coin's duplicitous references to elsewhere, as a supplemented and therefore ungrounded image. This second aspect of the penny's image haunts its value — a haunting that the stability of the penny's references to external powers attempts to repress. However, rather than begin to speculate about ghostly queens, one need not look further for this haunting than to the very materiality of the penny as a physical object. As Maurice Blanchot writes in his essay "Two Versions of the Imaginary," "the act of haunting is not the unreal visitation of the idea: what haunts is the inaccessible which one cannot rid oneself of, what one does not find and what, because of that, does not allow one to avoid it" (Blanchot 1999, 422). In other words, the inaccessibility of the basis of value — covered over by the ghostly image of the queen, no longer whom she was — is the second image, or the second 'version' of the image shown by the penny. It is what underlies the first image, as its bare, non-signifying matter, both more fundamental and less foundational than the ideal value that it is purported to uphold.

Blanchot describes the image as a 'present absence.' It is "an indifferent depth where nothing is affirmed" (Blanchot 1999, 417). However, this is hardly to be understood as some metaphysical depth, inaccessible because it is sitting somewhere high up in Plato's world of forms. The image is distant from the object, but again in two reciprocal senses, both of which take their impetus from its materiality. On the one hand, there is an image of value represented by the object: a penny represents one cent of monetary value. This distance is closed by the imposition of a larger system of value upon the penny, which then acts metonymically for its entire system of currency. On the other hand, the real force of the image arises from the distance that the object consistently replaces between itself, materially, and the linguistic or economic (i.e. formal) values that are imposed upon it. In other words, the object in a sense always maintains an impersonal distance from itself. Blanchot writes,

> After the object comes the image. 'After' means that first the thing must move away in order to allow itself to be grasped again. But that distancing is not the simple change of place of a moving object, which nevertheless remains the same. Here the distancing is at the heart of the thing… graspable because ungraspable, appearing as something that has disappeared, the return of what does not come back, the strange heart of the distance as the life and unique heart of the thing (Blanchot 1999, 418).

He then likens this distance inherent in the image to a cadaver, the radical indifference of which returns to haunt the world of the living (Blanchot 1999, 421). Because the penny depends on its image's reference to an external authority, such a cadaverous distance irrupts between its value and its status as an object.

The cadaver is no longer a person, but neither is it merely inorganic matter. Somehow, while it continues to evoke the emotions and memories of the person it once was, the cadaver remains potent in its indifference. The dead's inability to any longer respond makes itself felt as an absence, a void, which wrenches the witness of the dead from her relations with the world of the living, with the world of society in which finitude is forgotten, as well as with the determinate categories through which the world is understood. In their strangeness, the dead in this sense become undead. Blanchot writes that "[t]he cadaver is reflection making itself master of the reflected life, absorbing it, substantially identifying itself with it by making it lose its value in terms of use and truth and change into something incredible—unusual and neutral" (ibid). This is to say that the image functions as an unusual neutrality that cannot immediately be put to use, and that, as a result, imposes itself from somewhere outside of any regime of instrumental sense, meaning, or value. The image hovers between the living and the dead, the conceptual and the material, but originates from neither. The image on the penny is no exception, and so the queen then functions as this cadaverous, absent force that reveals the materiality of the penny as foreign to its value at the same time that it performs the guarantee of that value.

This dual aspect of the image of the penny prevents it from being placed entirely inside or outside of regimes of sense; it exists contradictorily between its material and signifying situations. The penny's image is engraved in the coin, and signifies more than its copper; it therefore cannot be considered as merely inert material. But because it is engraved upon this material, it is not only conceptual. Rather, existing ambiguously between these two poles, the image is spectral. It precludes its own interpretation, murmuring between signification and silence. However, at present the penny's circulation within a larger system of exchange recuperates its image, into which this system condenses and displaces itself, masking the image's ambivalence and imposing upon the penny a determinate value.

Writing on George Bataille's essay "The Pineal Eye," philosopher Rodolphe Gasché also theorizes the image as phantasmatic, locating its origin, or non-origin, in a movement through which its ambiguity is reduced for the sake of knowledge. For Gasché, the origin of the phantasm "is inscribed in its own scene. Therefore, the genetic question is impossible" (Gasché 2012, 145). This is to say that the material basis of the image is not separate from its appearance — or rather its dis-appearance — as the disruption of its own signification. Of the phantasmatic image, then, Gasché writes that it "does not denote some kind of a sensible fullness, as appears to be the case for the kind of image that, on the level of consciousness, is opposed to the empty concept. To the contrary, it replaces, misplaces, and distorts" (Gasché 2012, 127). For Gasché and Bataille, it is only through the restriction of these distortive aspects of the image that objective knowledge and value can be established. Put more specifically in terms of the penny, the money-form must restrict the image to merely its representational aspect in order to establish its regime of value.

General Economy, the Queen of England, and Surrealism

This repression of the spectral aspect of the image gives rise to what Bataille calls 'restricted economy.' In specifically political-economic terms, he writes:

> Economic science merely generalizes the isolated situation; it restricts its object to operations carried out with a view to a limited end, that of economic man. It does not take into consideration a play of energy that no particular end limits: the play of *living matter in general*…energy is always in excess (Bataille 1989, 23).

Bataille situates 'restricted economy' in opposition to the concept of a 'general economy.' Briefly, general economy is characterized by an acknowledgement of the complexity and overdetermination of any system of value and meaning. This is to say that there is always a general surplus of input that is lost in the creation of any restricted system, and so Bataille theorizes general economy as a way to address this problem of loss. Here these concepts can be useful for exploring some implications that the image of the penny carries with it, especially in relation to its disappearance from circulation.

As has been noted already, because the money-form restricts the penny from the more expansive possible relations of its material existence, to exist as a determinate unit of value, the penny can fairly definitively be said to participate in a restricted economy. The money-form precludes a general acknowledgement of the matter that is the penny's real basis, so as to naturalize its system of value, covering over the ambiguous material image of the penny with the positive image of monetary value. To remove the Canadian penny from circulation will then, at least in part, remove it from its place within this restricted economy. This de-circulation of the penny removes the secondary, appropriative image of the queen that supplements it with exchange value, revealing this value as a restriction that is arbitrary at best, and authoritarian at worst. The face of the queen, once mainstay of an imperial value, becomes a ghost trapped in the senseless materiality of the coin. She becomes Blanchot's corpse: a face that simultaneously has been removed from our world of signification, but which cannot merely be treated as inert matter. She becomes Gasché's phantasm, which interrupts the ideal restrictions of the money-form in order to temporarily open up a wellspring of the distortions inherent in the material image, unsettling objective systems of meaning and value. This, of course, is why the Canadian government, for its own sake, wants to collect and melt its pennies as fast as possible, incinerating its own former queen rather than rendering her a symbol of the ungroundedness of its economic practices. Devoid of value, the pennies that survive this mass melting will become symbols of what economy excludes. As such, they will embody the primary and indeterminate images upon which economy determines itself, and that it ultimately must reject in order to establish its restrictions.

Further, if pennies no longer circulate, and therefore are not actually able to present directly this uncanny material image of the groundlessness of monetary exchange, it should be remembered that credit and debit transactions still retain the one-cent value. This provides a more lasting and visible rupture in the otherwise naturalized continuity between the materiality of money and its restricted, ideal values. The penny, then, as the future absence of cents (and sense) between cash and credit economies, literally does haunt economics as a present absence, as the ghost of an acephalous queen, beheaded for the sake of masking the empty prosopopeia of the money-form and its inherent contradiction: that between its ideality and its materiality, between its two competing images, one of which restricts the other.

The non-circulated penny might then serve as what André Breton and Salvador Dalì called a 'surrealist object.' These are objects in which one attempts to materialize the subversion of the ego by the id—or, what is a similar thing, the subversion of meaning with non-meaning. As an example, Breton discusses a book of which he dreamt, that had a wooden gnome as a spine, among other features (Breton 1969, 277). Or, in Dalì's case, consider his 1935 painting *Paranoiac Visage* in which what at first appears to be the image of a face dissolves into a group of people, defying the viewer's attempt to reconstruct the painting's initial appearance. Or, again, there is the famous Lautréamontian image of a "chance meeting of an umbrella and a sewing machine upon an operating table," in which objects are removed from their usual contexts and rendered useless, thereby providing a critique of the bourgeois notions of instrumentality and productivity. These surrealist objects function as sorts of differentials between restricted and general economies, in that they transfer the restricted meanings and uses of objects into the nonsense of the matter from which they are composed. The penny—or at least the lacuna that it will leave between the ideal and material aspects of economics—will in turn become a surrealist object in this specific sense. In other words, the image of the penny's non-circulation will be the specter of the generality that economics initially contradicts and tries to escape, but cannot. Its disappearance marks the repressive and restrictive functioning of economic systems in general, while also demonstrating the weak points of these systems. The question then becomes one of utilizing the images of these weak points to facilitate economic change.

The Passport and the Holder

Hannah Jocelyn

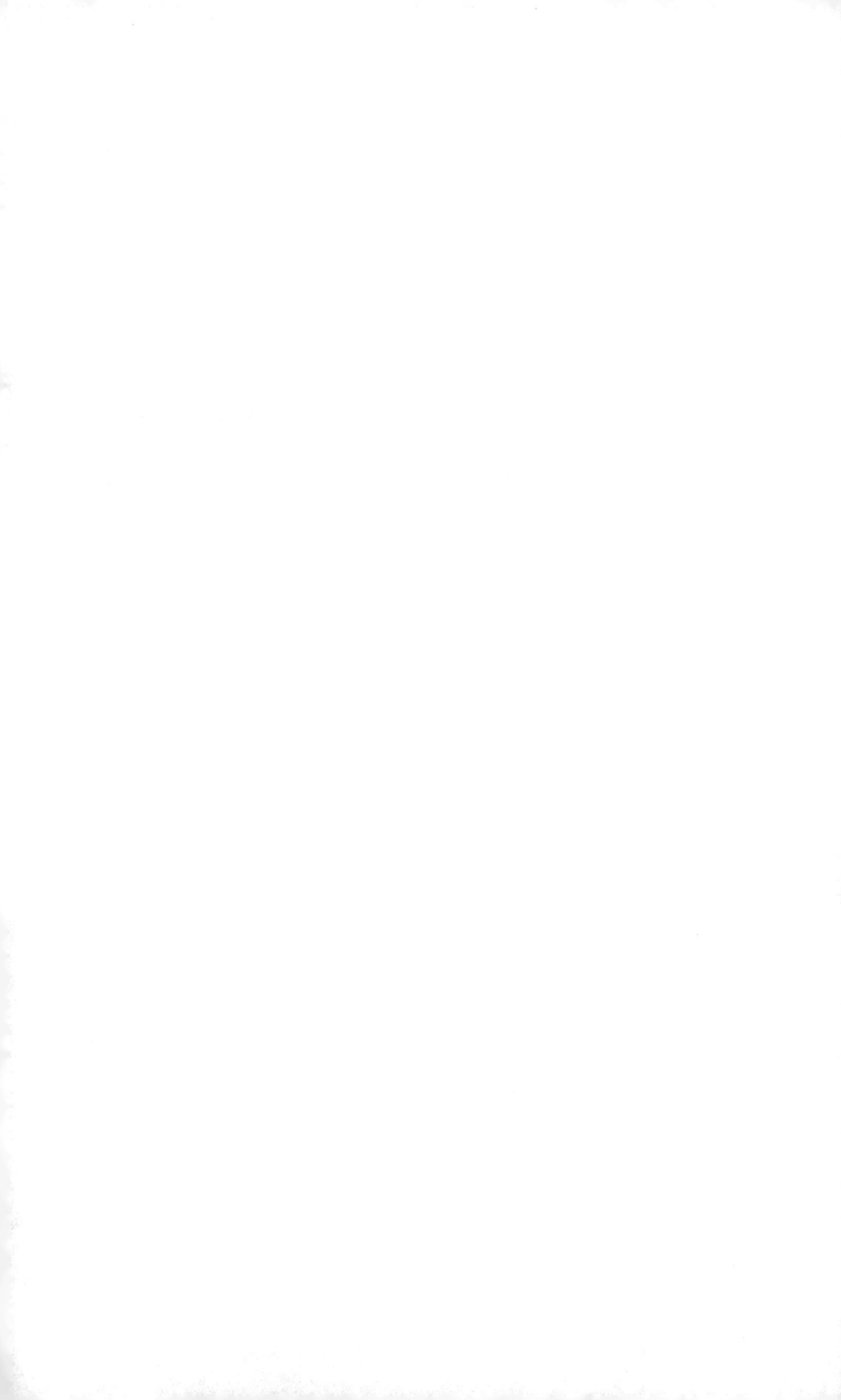

The Passport and the Holder

Hannah Jocelyn

In this evermore globalized and regulated world, owning a passport is seemingly ubiquitous. Whether a person is an international traveler or not, the passport has become as necessary as a birth certificate. It is an indicator of status, of mobility, and of belonging. This object, however, is not merely a claim to nationality, a record of journey, or a permit home. While it may be the device with which one can cross boundaries, it is also the device that erects them. The passport appears to offer freedom, but it in truth restricts and regulates movement. To be without a passport is to be constricted, denied access, denied legitimacy. To hold a passport, however, is not to avoid constriction. As a holder, one must accept governmental management, subject at all times to scrutiny in the name of security. The passport is a socially constructed device that, without our having collectively agreed to its meaning, would be nothing more than an unflattering picture. As it is, the passport holds issues of freedom, identity, exclusion, transnationalism, security, and more. We must question, then, what we have collectively agreed upon.

A Brief History

The word 'passport' derives from the French words *passer*—meaning to go, pass, or proceed—and *port*—meaning harbor, or wear—which refer to "a range of travel documents and letters of permission which both eased travel for individuals and allowed governments to oversee mobility and control dissidence" (Higgins and Leps 1998, 98). Early conceptions of passports were other types of documents called 'safe conduct' papers that secured safe passage, and 'king's licenses' which granted permission to leave a territory (Robertson 2010, 3).[20] These early documents of course had no photograph, and thus carried with them the assumption that the bearer was the person named in the document. The interpreter had to trust that the holder was true to his identity claim. In his book, *The Passport in America: The History of a Document*, Craig Robertson suggests that two significant developments at the end of the eighteenth century were particularly critical to the evolution of the passport from these essentially unproven passage papers into our modern passport. The first development was the blossoming geopolitical importance of the nation-state (Ibid, 4). When states began to self-govern within the sovereign nation, the passport became necessary to monitor the movement of citizens. In this way, Eric Neumayer points out that our contemporary surveillance system is "inextricably linked to the evolution of the modern nation-state" (Neumayer 2006, 3). The second development was "the appearance throughout the nineteenth century of claims to objectivity in the production of knowledge, particularly via the contested emergence of scientific and bureaucratic practices" (Robertson 2010, 4). Anxiety surrounding these practices made a standard mode of keeping record imperative. A person's word could no longer be proof enough of his identity. These developments, Robertson proposes, "contributed to the process through which identity and identification became a problem for which the passport was seen as a solution" (Ibid). The passport offered a trustworthy way to monitor the citizens of the emerging nation-state. Despite this evolution, the passport was not immediately universal.

In 1782, the Continental Congress gave the Department of Foreign Affairs the responsibility of issuing passports in the name of the United States. Almost thirty years later, the first passports that included a description of the holder were granted, proof that he was who he claimed to be. Yet, during this era fewer than one hundred passports were issued annually. Most citizens remained unknown to the federal government, except possibly as a census number (Robertson 2010, 6). The need to be identified operated at a mostly local level. As Robertson writes, "the limited sphere in which people traveled, and significantly in which business occurred, meant that it was rare that the need for identification could not be satisfied by personal knowledge or reputation" (Ibid). For the most part, business was conducted between acquaintances. Twenty years later, the number of passports issued annually had increased tenfold and twenty years after that, Congress passed a law which decreed that passports should be issued only to citizens. Simultaneously, a fee for acquiring the passport was introduced, climbing steadily from one dollar since then. By the end of the nineteenth century, when businesses enlarged and began to be conducted on a more national scale, credit reporting was a necessary supplement to the limitations of personal recognition— the passport was used to substantiate claims of good credit. Herein was "one of the first nationally based bureaucratic surveillance systems," (Ibid) physically embodied by the passport object. The passport became "a legal and factual necessity" (Parker 1954, 865) in North America when, in 1918, impelled in part by the First World War, a law was passed which made passports mandatory, or "a lawful prerequisite to travel *to* foreign countries" (Ibid). This perceived necessity has endured ever since, exponentially expanding in ubiquitousness.

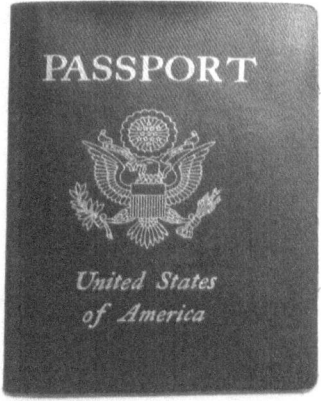 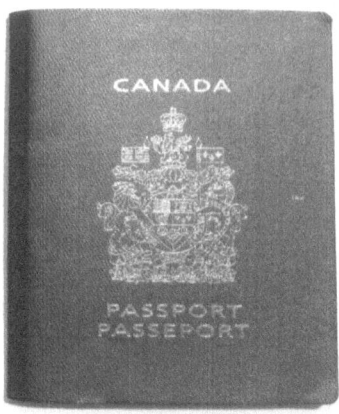

Figure 1. <u>Passports of the United States of America and Canada</u>. Photograph by author. July 24, 2013.

The Coded Composition

In the United States, thirteen million passports were issued in the 2012 fiscal year alone, and close to one hundred and twelve million since 2005 (Travel State). This globally recognized document, "granted, in the name of a head of state, by an authorized agent, to a named individual," (Higgins and Leps 1998, 99) is a booklet decorated on the outside with a national government insignia (**Fig. 1**).

Inside the cover is a request that the holder be permitted (in the words of the United States passport) "to pass without delay or hinderance and in case of need to give all lawful aid and protection" by other governments when he or she is traveling in foreign countries. The inner page contains personal information about the holder, "obliged to be the person named by the document" (Ibid): name, photograph, date, place of birth, signature and a passport identification number, unique to every passport. The remaining pages, used for visas and entry/exit stamps, are empty when initially presented, but for decoration distinctive to the nation (**Fig. 2**).

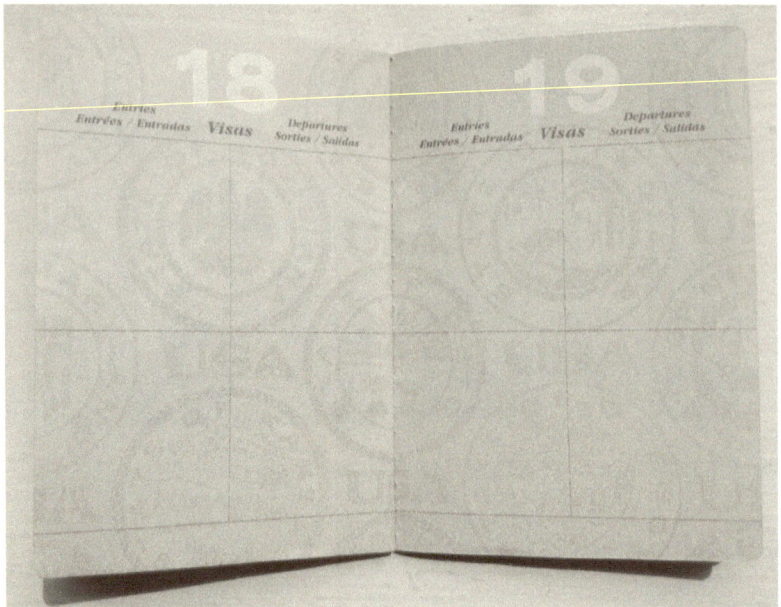

Figure 2. Inside of a United States of America passport. Photograph by author. July 24, 2013.

Throughout the booklet are various devices to prevent fraudulent passports from being created such as lamination, holograms, tamper proof paper, and so on. At a border, a uniformed guard inspects the passport, inspects the bearer, questions the bearer, and then deems him traversable or otherwise (Salter 2003, 123). This is the physical constitution and the activity of the passport that, as Mark Salter notes significantly in his book *Rights of Passage: The Passport in International Relations*, forever remains the property of the government and must be "surrendered" (**Fig. 3**) upon its request. This object is far from limited to its physical constitution, however. It is actively coded.

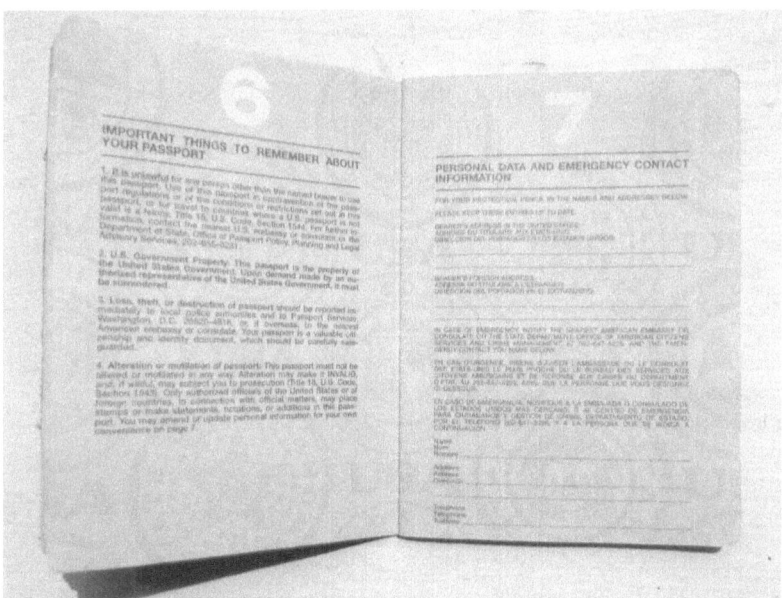

Figure 3. Inside of a United States of America passport. Photograph by author. July 24, 2013.

Systematized Exclusions

The passport not only tells the interpreter (a word used purposefully here, one who *interprets* the inscribed signs) where a person is from, has been, and belongs; it is a presumed certification of identity (Salter 2003, 96). It is a promise to other sovereign nations that the holder is, to use Salter's words, a "safe and legitimate traveler—because she has a home to which she can be returned," (Ibid, 4) guaranteeing "that those denied access can be sent back to the issuing country" (Neumayer 2006, 11). Safe and legitimate in the case of passports means free of disease, free of state harming agenda, free of incriminating record. In the promise of safety and legitimacy are wrapped the multiple concerns about freedom of movement and security, economic fluidity between countries, and safeguarding boundaries. Thomas J. Biersteker suggests in his article "The Rebordering of North America? Implications for Conceptualizing Borders after September 11" that the passport was an answer to the question: "How could the need for physical security, protection from violence be balanced by the need to maintain an open economic and commercial border that promised both economic security and the benefits of a continuation of expanded commerce?" (Biersteker 2003, 153). The passport is therefore the object around which these competing concerns are organized. It is how they are reconciled. Operating, as Salter writes, "at the nexus of the desire for wealth and mobility and the fear of violence and mobility," (Salter 2003, 160) the passport—and the promise therein—ensures that the holder can travel without violating security, without threatening violence.

However, what of the person who does not hold a passport? Not only do passports cost over $100 to secure and therefore are out of reach for many impoverished persons, but governments reserve the right to withhold a passport, often in the guise of protecting the state. In some instances, documentation is refused, regardless of citizenship, from persons who are deemed a threat for having committed or been charged with or convicted of an offense. As just one example of many, José Padilla, who was arrested at the Chicago O'Hare International Airport on May 8, 2002 by a U.S. Customs officer, had been previously convicted of conspiracy charges (Chesney and Wittes 2013). Upon arrest, he was declared an 'enemy combatant' under the Authorization for the Use of Military Force (AUMF) so as to be denied his rights as a U.S. citizen (Salter 2003, 128). Documentation has also historically been refused from persons who are seen as unfavorable, such as if they are associated with a disease considered hazardous to the health of the body politic for example. In the late 1980s, upon the recommendation of the U.S. Centers for Disease Control and Prevention, the United States banned non-citizens with HIV/AIDS from entering the country (Ibid, 65). As Higgins and Leps write,

> Each state retains the authority to dispense travel documents (passports, visas, work permits) at will, simply through bureaucratic regulations, and thereby reserves the right to locate and control individuals and peoples according to the changing demands of economic, social, and political contingencies (Higgins and Leps 1998, 95).

In other words, by maintaining charge over who is and is not granted a passport, the state asserts management over every person as well as every border. Thus, being the foremost document used for border crossing, passports are as much a contemporary necessity for travel as they are for identification. They function as a crucial mechanism for "the 'first line of defense' against the entry of undesirables" (Neumayer 2006, 9). If the bearer can be identified by his passport as someone who is a threat to national security or health, then he will be denied access.

In his article, "(Dis)qualified Bodies: Securitization, Citizenship and 'Identity Management,'" Benjamin J. Muller notes that the passport as an authorization for movement is "allegedly purged of the ugly politics of us and them, friends and enemies, inclusion and exclusion" (Muller 2005). That is to say, it is intended to be unbiased and depolarizing. Rather than an arbitrary prohibition of undesirables, the passport offers a "securitized, bureaucratized and 'scientized' realm of identity management" (Ibid) ostensibly rid of prejudice of any kind. Muller suggests that it "provides a seemingly sanitary means of identifying/authenticating threats" (Ibid). Yet despite *seeming* sanitary and unbiased, a biased exclusion still occurs. No matter how bureaucratic or putatively impartial, if a state accepts certain people and rejects others, a divisive system prevails. A distinction between safety and danger, legitimate and illegitimate identities ineluctably exists, not to mention a socioeconomic bifurcation. Passports, the material object of this 'identity management,' authorize access to or debarring from assets, amenities, and areas. As Neumayer notes, "facilitating the mobility of some is achieved at the expense of inhibiting and deterring mobility of others" (Neumayer 2006, 5-6). Thus, passports divide people into two categories: holders and non-holders. The holder is sanctioned for free movement, approved as an upstanding citizen with an authentic identity, who belongs to a nation while the non-holder cannot permissibly cross borders, does not bear evidence of his legitimacy, does not belong. There exists, therefore, a hierarchy of citizenship, tiered by holders and non-holders.

Crossing and Creating Borders

While the passport inherently claims to be an instrument of free movement—the ticket to come and go—it actually contains and constructs boundaries. In promising security, allowing safe passage, the passport also erects limitations and generates state custody of citizen movement. In his book *The Invention of the Passport: Surveillance, Citizenship and the State,* John Torpey purports that the passport produces, reproduces, enforces, and reinforces a monopolization of the "means of movement" (Torpey 2000, 4). He writes that this monopoly on movement, predicated on the emergence of the passport and governed in the United States by the network of Homeland Security and border patrol, created:

> The codification of laws establishing which types of persons may move within or cross their borders, and determining how, when, and where they may do so; the stimulation of the worldwide development of techniques for uniquely and unambiguously identifying each and every person on the face of the globe, from birth to death; the construction of bureaucracies designed to implement this regime of identification and to scrutinize persons and documents in order to verify identities; and the creation of a body of legal norms designed to adjudicate claims by individuals to entry into particular spaces and territories (Ibid, 7).

It engenders, in other words, a system of recognition and recording, wrapped in regulation over which the state has total command. This system is a boundary both holders and non-holders must negotiate. The passport is the primary object of this monopolized structure. Depriving people of the "freedom to move across certain spaces" is to "render them dependent on states and the state system for the authorization to do so" (Ibid, 4). People become "dependent on states for the possession of an 'identity' from which they can escape only with difficulty and which may significantly shape their access to various spaces" (ibid). Without passports, individuals cannot leave the United States with any certainty of being able to return. Significantly, some fourteen million undocumented people, many of whom have lived in the United States for nearly all their lives, must live with this uncertainty (Meyer 2009, 77). On the other hand, although citizens holding passports have the luxury of mobility, access, and authenticity, they have also fully surrendered themselves to, in Karl E. Meyer's words, the "unlimited power of the state." (Meyer cited in Salter 2003, 127). The use of passports has "the definite effect of making all individuals potential aliens who must bear the marks of state identification in order to exercise the *inalienable* human right to mobility" (Higgins and Leps 1998, 108). The passport, then, constructs restraints in its very existence, contrary to its claim of offering free movement. The holder is not free, a subject of the state system that exercises a monopoly on movement. The non-holder is not free, excluded from the rights (however monitored) the passport allows.

The vitality of the passport developed out of state need to document the identity of each citizen, out of economic need to be sure of good credit, and out of national need to secure and protect its borders. Not just an unbecoming photograph, a list of representative markers, a few pages for stamps, not merely a document which legally identifies its holder, connecting him to a nation, the passport is an object that at once constructs boundaries and makes them permeable, includes and excludes, produces identity and limits it. Holders are subjugated by the state while non-holders are excluded from it. With developments such as NEXUS passes, CANPASS, and Global Entry, the future of the passport seems to be an evolution into biometric credit cards. Such a trajectory is sure to streamline the hierarchization between holders and non-holders. Improving this technology will serve only to affirm that power is not in the hands of the holder, but in the hands of the granter.

Corinne
Thiessen Hepher

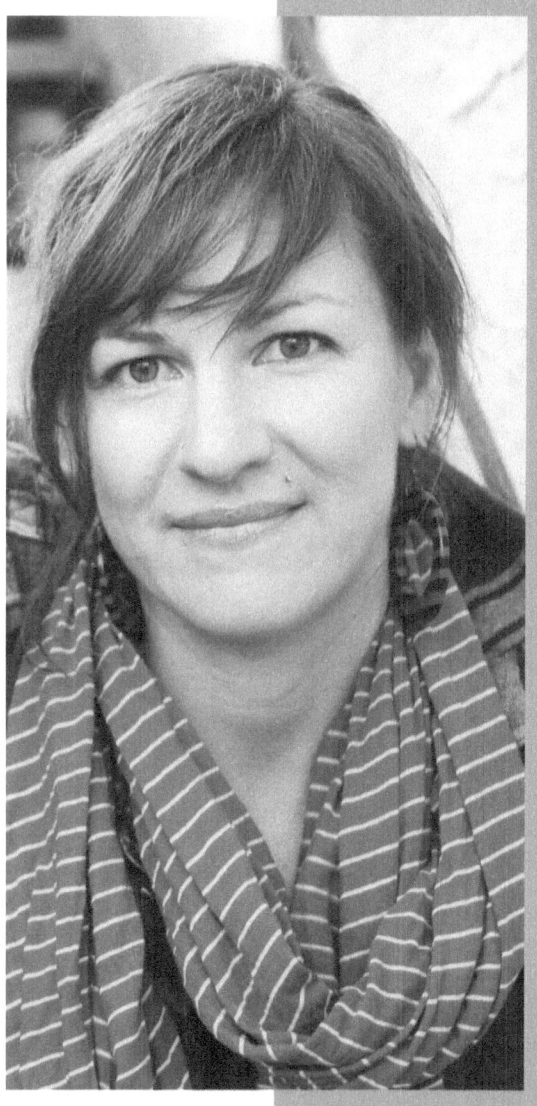

Gleaning Gendered Objects: Hybrid Bodies and the Radical Potential of the Grotesque

Corinne Thiessen Hepher

My art practice has evolved from collecting and reassembling found objects, to incorporating those objects into an exploration of the grotesque, to reinterpreting historical objects used for disciplinary and corrective treatments. Through kinetic sculptures, drawing, performance, and video installation, I look at the significance of objects in relation to constructions of *otherness* through a feminist lens. Prosthetics and body restraints in various works function as a metaphor for contemporary conditions of social constraint, silencing, and powerlessness. I introduce feminist theories on gendered objects that have informed my current practice, followed by a discussion of various conceptions of the grotesque, and an historical examination of objects intended to enhance, control, or correct.

At the heart of this discussion is the feminist challenge to the mind/body split articulated throughout Western theoretical discourse. Feminist and cultural theorists suggest that the oppression of *others* is based on the mind/body dualism idealized in the Cartesian modern subject. This dichotomy is hierarchical, privileging mind over body. In it, the body is associated with the feminine, the animal, and with nature, and is to be transcended or overcome (Grosz 1994, 4). This exclusive and oppressive hierarchy is my impetus for exploring processes of subversion and reclamation in my research and material practice.

Gendered Objects and *Others*

I initially approach art making by collecting and amassing everyday objects and images in an attempt to unearth taxonomies of gender and constructions of feminine social identity. I ask the questions: what does it mean for an object to be gendered? Does the object contribute to constructions of binary identifications? Objects and images from popular culture influence gender identification through socialization. They saturate our visual environment and structure our knowledge of others, the world, and ourselves (Wagner-Ott 2002, 246).

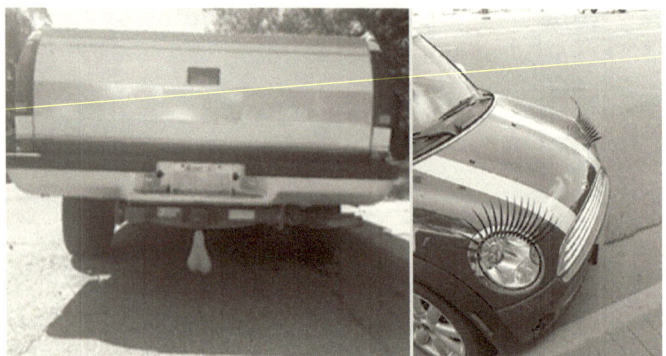

'Truck Nutz' and 'Eyelashes for Cars' are examples of gendered objects or stereotypes. Photographs by Corinne Thiessen Hepher (left) and Melanie Marie (right), 2013.

I therefore collect discarded objects and ephemera such as birth control pill packaging, pregnancy tests, tampon insertion instructions, and other objects that reference biological processes. Objects culturally coded as 'feminine,' such as plastic curlers and pantyhose, are repurposed in several of my sculptural works. The collection I have accumulated as part of my practice provides me with the material to excavate, examine, and classify gendered objects and their role in the enhancement, correction, and control of women's bodies and behaviour.

In my work *Common Errors Post-Excavation* (2010) (**Fig.1**), acting as 'imposter archaeologist,' I begin reassembling found items such as nylon pantyhose and plastic hair curlers. The following questions inform this work: if objects are rearranged incorrectly and/or outside of their intended context, what are the consequences? What assumptions of empirical knowledge do we take as historical 'fact'? What can be learned from past anthropological methodologies and the medical or scientific treatment of human subjects? In what way do current medical and psychoanalytical models pathologize 'abnormal' bodies and behaviours through the language of 'disease'?

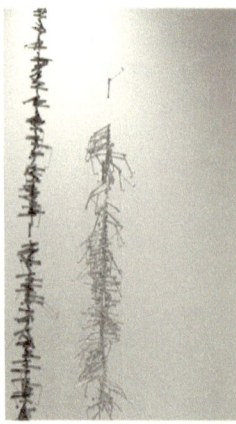
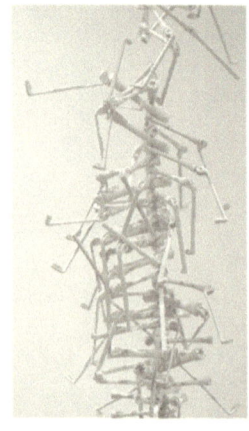

Figure 1. Corinne Thiessen Hepher, *Common Errors Post-Excavation,* 2010. Courtesy of the artist.

Gleaning rejected objects allowed me to examine which objects are privileged and why. My interest in the margins (including underprivileged *others*) leads to an examination of the relationship between objects and bodies and their economic, social, cultural, and political implications. Collecting objects, images, and ideas that are culturally peripheral, prompts an inquiry into the grotesque, the abject, and formlessness (*informe*).

The Grotesque and the Monstrous: Theoretical Introductions

The grotesque is often portrayed as deformed, hybrid, or metamorphic (Conelly 2011, 3), with ambiguous gender and bodily excess. Associated with "the earth, corrupted flesh, the sexual, and the scatological," the grotesque can include plant, animal, and human imagery (Ibid, 1). Grotesque imagery includes ugly, monstrous hybrid caricatures such as the centaur, griffin, Minotaur, satyr, and sphinx (Ibid, 2). While the classical body – transcendent, monumental, closed, static, self-contained, symmetrical, rational and individual – is the ideal of the high culture of the Renaissance, the grotesque body, on the other hand, is open, protruding, irregular, secreting, multiple, changing, low, and carnivalesque (Russo 1994, 8).

Because of this bodily openness and interconnectedness, Sarah Cohen Shabot defends the grotesque as an important site for the new, embodied, postmodern subject (Shabot 2007, 57). Being unfinished, lacking clearly defined boundaries (Bakhtin 1984, 26), and ambiguously gendered (de-sexualized or hyper-sexualized), the grotesque allows for an undermining of the Cartesian pure mind.

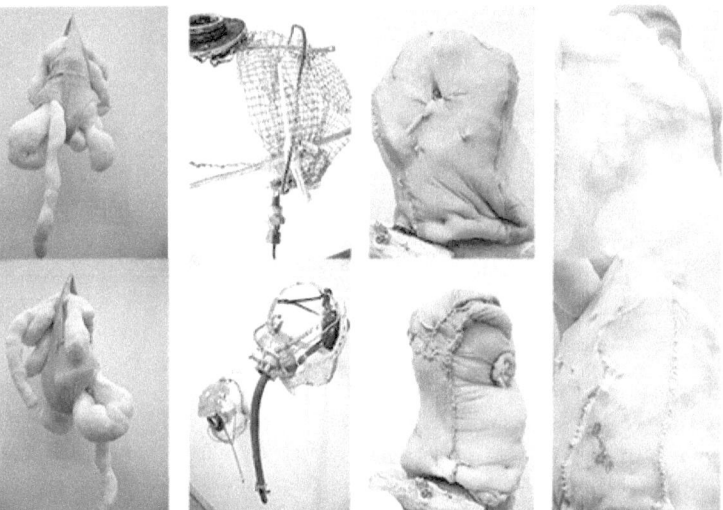

Corinne Thiessen Hepher, *Untitled*, 2012, 2013, studio production. Courtesy of the artist.

These studio works experiment with 'gendered' materials and ideas about containment, restraint hybrid forms, and the body using found objects: nylon pantyhose, polyester fill, underwear, scrap aluminum, plastic hair curlers, hosing, glass eye, embroidery floss, thread.

The Hybrid Grotesque: Theoretical Investigations and Material Practice

In the work *Interrupture* (2011) (**Fig. 2**), I employ the hybrid aspect of the grotesque. The work is comprised of a bodysuit that is constructed from nylon pantyhose and polyester fill and can be worn on the body. The protruding limbs, like prosthetic tentacles, resemble ambiguous genitalia. While it was initially intended as a sculptural object, I wore the suit in a swimming pool and documented the performance as a video recording. By placing my body in the work, I 'transformed' myself into a hybrid imaginary being.

Underwater, the body extension had the appearance of providing superhuman ability, but in fact dangerously inhibited my ability to move. During the recording of the performance, I shared the pool with a competitive swim team who, for unknown reasons, physically collided with me at one point. I suspect that my presence was not welcome in their practice area, or they refused to deviate from their course. I was delighted to include this 'mistake' - the collision between human and beast - in the narrative because it appears as though the beast is ravaging or consuming the swimmer. It also amplifies the differences between the 'freak' outsider and the synchronized, uniform team.

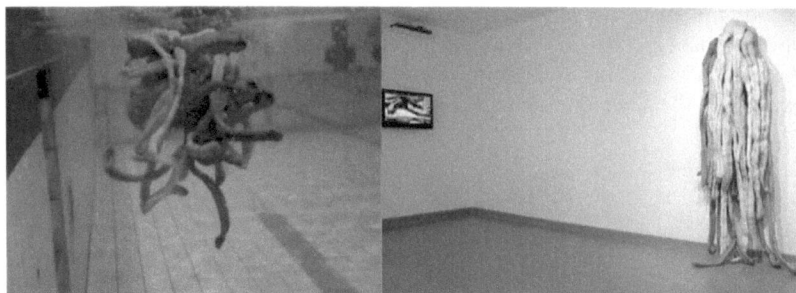

Figure 2. Corinne Thiessen Hepher, *Interrupture*, 2010. Courtesy of the artist.

Likewise, the work *Miranda*, (2012) (**Fig.3**), incorporates the hybrid grotesque, as machine, animal, and human representations are ambiguously merged. The sculpture consists of a plaster and foam human midsection (torso) that is cast from my body, from waist to upper leg. An articulating wooden tail protrudes from the lower back near the buttocks. A 12-volt electrical motor is secured to the 'body' and powers the tail in a circular motion. The tail becomes rigid and then flaccid with each rotation.

Miranda is inspired by the fictional novel *Geek Love* by Katherine Dunn, which tells the story of the Binewski family, whose travelling circus, the 'Carnival Fabulon,' stays in business with the help of their deformed, 'freak' children who were physically mutated by the chemicals and radio isotopes ingested by their mother during pregnancy. The Carnival Fabulon is a place where norms are abhorred and outsiders are regarded with suspicion. One night, a hunchbacked albino dwarf, discovers the otherwise 'normal' Miranda onstage at a strip club, exposing her small tail.

The tail in *Miranda* (2012) is an example of excess: a characteristic of the grotesque. Physiological anomalies, described in medical literature as malformations, deformations, anatomical curiosities, or 'cosmetic stigma,' (Mukhopadhyay 23, 2012) expose ideas about non-normative bodies and show how language, history, social context, and other factors determine whether an attribute will be valued or viewed as a congenital defect.

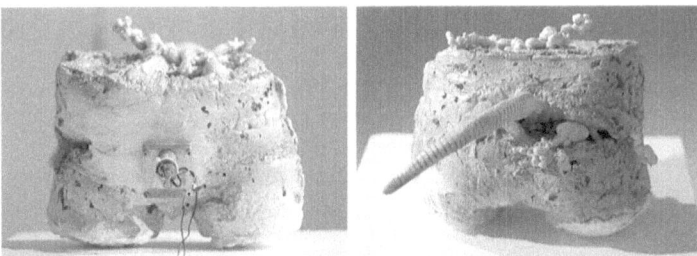

Figure 3. Corinne Thiessen Hepher, *Miranda*, 2012. Courtesy of the artist.

The hybrid grotesque is also considered in the work *Hot Tail* (2012) (**Fig. 4**). *Hot Tail* was a storefront window[21] performance where three live performers and five animated sculptural objects moved in a rigid rhythmic choreography triggered by the viewer. Five human midsections, cast in plaster and foam (similar in form to the work *Miranda* described above), stood in front of the human performers. The viewers outside triggered a motion sensor and activated the entire production. The performers were instructed to move only when the machines powered up and the lights started flashing. The performers, with their backs to the viewers, swayed in a left-right motion, causing their identical wooden tails to swing back and forth in unison. The viewers controlled the production: through their voyeuristic curiosity, they initiated the 'red light freak show,'[22] activating the push/pull, seduction/repulsion characteristic of the grotesque.

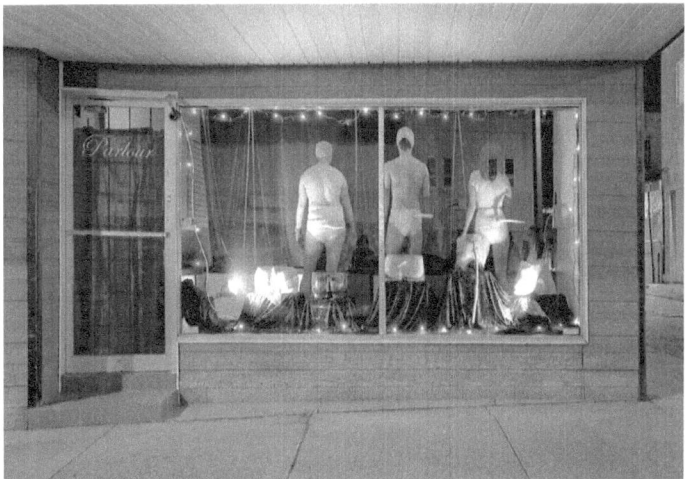

Figure 4. Corinne Thiessen Hepher, *Hot Tail*, 2012. Courtesy of the artist.

In the performance *Metamorphosis* (2012) (**Fig.5**), I continued my exploration of hybridity and metamorphosis inspired by Franz Kafka's novella of the same name.[23] During the performance, I acted out a series of rituals by binding and strapping my limbs into 'insect legs' while suspended from the ceiling in a canvas harness. The insect legs were constructed from tree branches, joined by hinges similar to a marionette hinge. For the duration of the performance, I emitted a variety of high-pitched screams, screeches, and other vocalizations while 'transforming' into an insect, performing 'madness' and acting 'hysterical.' By performing unruly, inappropriate behaviours, I intended to question the historical construction of women's 'diseases' and the out-of-control body.

My vocalizations mimicked the performances of the 'hysterics' in the Salpêtrière Asylum in Paris, France.[24] Jean-Martin Charcot, the influential professor of clinical diseases of the nervous system who diagnosed and analyzed female patients suffering from 'hysteria,' encouraged a sense of theatricality at the Salpêtrière. Patients 'acted' their hysteria as they performed 'erotic misbehaviour' (Justice-Malloy 1995, 134) in front of the camera for a photographic publication (Ibid). It also seemed patients learned hysterical movements, gestures, and vocalizations after they entered the Salpêtrière. Charcot sometimes had his patients dress in costume as he delivered lectures at the hospital amphitheatre to audiences intrigued by the hypnotized hysteric (Ibid, 135). Due to the prevalence of the disease and the growing interest in hysteria, Charcot and other physicians began to diagnose patients more frequently simply because they were seeking and expecting to find hysterical symptoms. This contributed to speculation about the validity of the disease (Ibid, 136).

The medicalization of the female body, which was seen as 'susceptible' to hysteria, is reified through discourses in science and medicine, psychoanalysis, and institutionalized social relations according to Foucault and reiterated by Anne Balsamo (Balsamo 1996, 20). In this way, language and communication perpetuate accepted hegemonic ideologies about disease and deviant bodies. These power relations - a collection of practices that produce cultural effects - operate to exercise control over the body (Ibid, 21). As such, taken for granted 'truths' about the hysterical female body, which were in fact culturally constructed and institutionalized, are now widely questioned (Ibid, 21).[25] Through my performance of unruly, awkward, erotic, and regressive vocalizations and movements, *Metamorphosis* drew attention to the historical pathologizing of women's sexuality and mental illness.

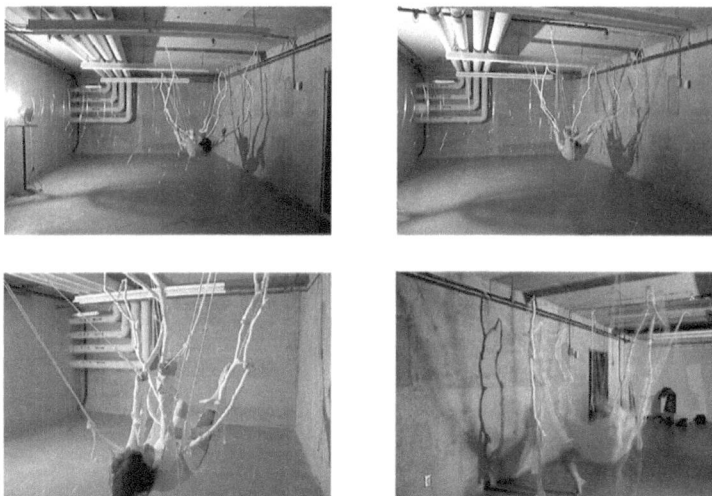

Figure 5. Corinne Thiessen Hepher, *Metamorphosis*, 2012. Courtesy of the artist.

To tie in the previously discussed grotesque body, and the performance of the out-of-control body in *Metamorphosis*, I look to Amelia Jones's argument for body art[26] to "dislocate or decenter the Cartesian subject of modernism" (Jones 1998, 1). The 'body/self' she describes, with all of its racial, gender, and sexual identifiers reveals "the hidden body that secured the authority of modernism" (Ibid, 14). By exposing the body and performing the exaggerations of sexual, ethnical, or other non-normative bodies, the artist dispels myths of the detached, universal, authoritative modern subject. In other words, our identities are never stable, closed, or static (as idealized in the Cartesian pure mind), but change, shift and morph, allowing us to blur the lines between self and (monstrous) *other*. Women, associated with the body in all of its unpredictability, share the threatening aspects of the monstrous and the grotesque. In this way, feminist artists appropriate the grotesque in their work as a method of undermining the separate, Cartesian ideal.

Informe/Formlessness: Spit, Slime, and Secretions

The excesses of the body, and the body that is uncontained, protruding, and open to the world (characteristic of the grotesque), find parallels in the *informe*. The *informe*, or formlessness, is described by Georges Bataille and expanded on by Yves Alain Bois and Rosalind Krauss in *Formless: A User's Guide*. Formlessness is not immaterial; rather, it includes everything that resides in the gutter, that which is discarded and disgusting. It includes base language such as swears and slang, socially unacceptable behaviours, and abject bodily detritus. It concerns that which does not make sense or add up. As with the grotesque, it resists fixed rules and categories. It is described as an uprooting or slippage of reason, a slide towards lowness. In this way, the *informe* is an attempt to bring things down (Bois and Krauss 1997, 16, 17).

With this in mind, I constructed *Drool Machine* or *Leak Body* (work in progress) (**Fig. 6**), a small sculptural object powered by an extremely slow (1rpm) motor. A reservoir of liquid drips intermittently from an orifice at the rear of the object, leaking a colourless, odourless fluid.

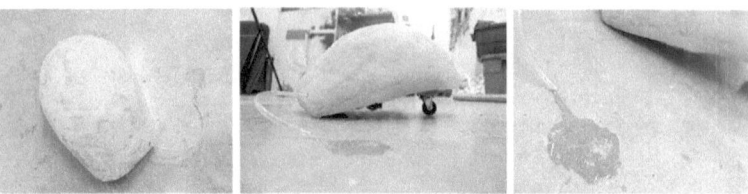

Figure 6. Corinne Thiessen Hepher, *Drool Machine or Leak Body* (work in progress), 2013. Courtesy of the artist.

Drool Machine incorporates hybridity, merging machine and body. It plays on the term 'snail trail,' a slang description of vaginal lubrication produced during female arousal. The slime or spittle produced by the *Drool Machine/Leak Body* is intended to be a witty and subversive undermining of the misogynist loathing of the (female) body.

Jean-Paul Sartre, according to Rosalind Krauss, articulates his disgust for the *visqueux* (slimy) and the female body that produces it. The *slimy* is neither solid nor liquid: "This flaccid ooze… does not have the resistance of solids; instead, as it clings stickily to the fingers, sucking at them, compromising them, it is docile." Sartre favours solids, which are like tools and can be taken up and put down again, having served their purpose. "But the slimy, in the form of the gagging suction of a leech-like past that will not release its grip, seems to contain its own form of possessiveness" (Krauss 1996, 92). Sartre characterizes slime as feminine: "yielding, clinging, sweet, passive, possessive" (Ibid). It is a substance that compromises the autonomous subject. "This idea of slime is a threat to autonomy and self-definition due to the suffocating nearness of the mother" (Ibid). Michel Leirus describes spittle as inconsistent with indefinite contours. It is imprecise in colour and humidity (Bois and Krauss 1997, 18). As such, spit is "unverifiable and non-hierarchized," which makes it the ideal concept to level hierarchies– "spit is the very symbol of the *informe*"(Ibid).

In other words, as a concept and a gendered object, slime is incorporated in *Drool Machine* to subversively undermine the privileging of solids, and the privileged modern subject idealized as rational and autonomous. This substance, neither solid nor liquid, is indecisive. It occupies a position of otherness, and resists the dichotomous privilege of mind over body, while it interrupts and disrupts autonomous control with the undeniable presence of the (out of control) body. The vulnerability of the body leaks out of the machine. The idea of leakage, precarious boundaries, fluid identities, and the resistance of fixed categories is realized in this work.

Building on the idea of the *informe* and corrective treatment methods, the project *Ortho Ensemble* (work in progress, 2013) (**Fig. 7 and 8**) includes facial restraints and corrective medical implements inspired by orthodontic headgear. Spoons, spatulas, pacifiers, candy and other household objects are incorporated into the wearable restraint to inhibit speech. Language is distorted as a metaphor for social compliance, communication ruptures, powerlessness, and silencing. Here, the mouth is compromised.

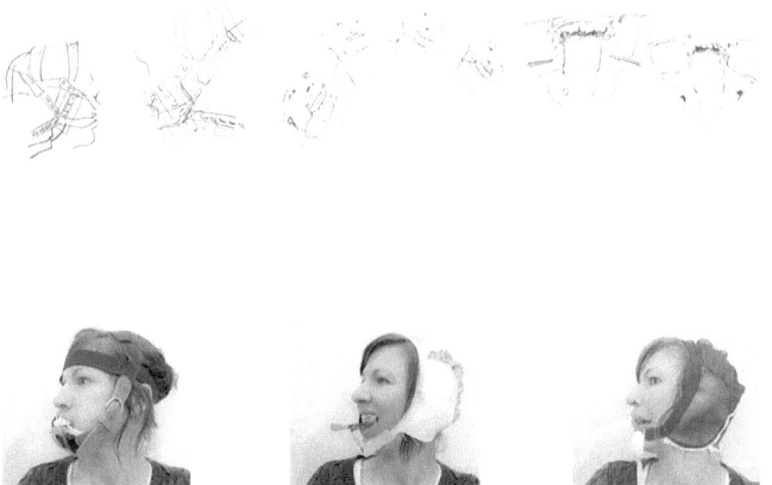

Figure 7. Corinne Thiessen Hepher, *headgear studies,* 2013. Courtesy of the artist.

Various volunteers sing or recite specific texts while wearing the homemade headgear. The texts concern ways in which people or groups are silenced.[27] Tying in the previous project on slime and spit, I draw connections to a text by Michel Leirus, referenced by Bois and Krauss. Spittle "...lowers the mouth – the visible sign of intelligence – to the level of the most shameful organs... given the identical source of language and spittle, any philosophical discourse can legitimately be figured by the incongruous image of the sputtering orator" (Bois and Krauss 1997, 18). Because Western culture has placed tremendous privilege on spoken language and has positioned language and speech as a sign of intelligence, *Ortho Ensemble* draws attention to speech that cannot be communicated because of conditions where autonomy is compromised. What is most important here is the struggle to say something you cannot say because of social or political silencing and threatening consequences.

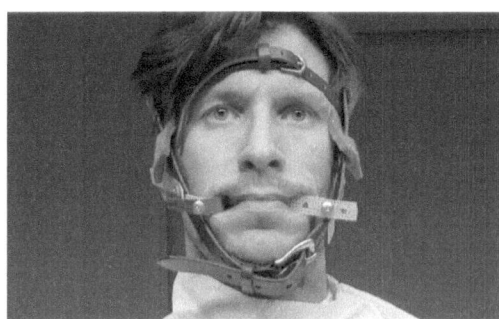

Figure 8. Corinne Thiessen Hepher, *Ortho Ensemble,* video still, 2013. Courtesy of the artist.

In one of the texts recorded for the 'headgear choir,' participants recite my grandmother's Second World War survival story. Just prior to Nazi occupation and eventual eviction, her Ukrainian village experienced the threat of Siberia: "…everybody was afraid… If you said something, and they didn't like that, then (*pffft*), off you went to Siberia. Not right away, but the next day…they came with black…vans, and took 'em away. We were very quiet. Everybody was quiet…"[28] By using an apparatus to impede speech, the objects of *Ortho Ensemble* act as metaphor for restriction and silencing enforced by institutional and political power structures.[29]

Among the many historical instruments of discipline and punishment for women, I am particularly interested in the brank or 'gossip's bridle.' The brank was a large metal headpiece that fit over a woman's face. A plate of iron placed in the mouth covered the tongue. The mouthpiece was either sharpened or covered with spikes. If the offender attempted to move her tongue in any way it was likely

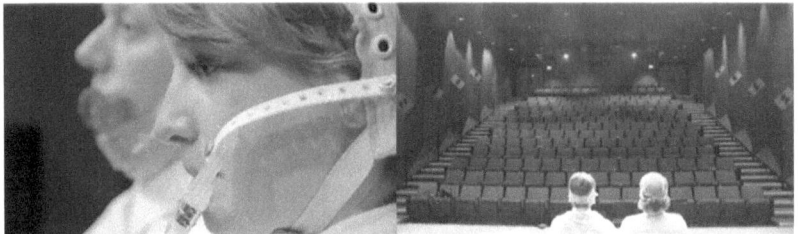

Figure 9. Corinne Thiessen Hepher, *Every Body Was Afraid*, video still, 2013. Courtesy of the artist.

to be injured (Andrews 1970, 38). The brank was administered for being noisy, swearing, or being argumentative. In the Middle Ages, 'scolds' were treated as offenders of the public peace as "the free use of the tongue gave rise to riots and feuds…."[30] Along with the 'Ducking Stool,' where women were strapped to chairs and lowered into cold rivers as punishment, the Mayor and Justice used the brank on women who were charged with street brawling or for insulting constables (Andrews 1970, 42). Placing the brank on the offending person was an elaborate process:

> The constable or other official, would then stand in front of his victim, and force the knife or plate A, into her mouth, the divided band passing on either side of her nose, which would protrude through the opening B. The hoop would then be closed behind, the band brought down from the top to the back of the head, and fastened down upon it, at E, and thus the cage would at once be firmly and immovably fixed so long as her tormentors might think fit. With the chain, she would be attached to a post or a wall (Andrews, 1970, 55).

The brank worked to silence women. The guilty woman might also have been led through the village with a chain, or in some cases, if she did not comply, she would be wheeled through the streets in a wheelbarrow. Sometimes the *threat* of the brank would be enough to keep women quiet.

While some argue that upholding norms is a critical aspect of society because deviant acts threaten social order (Adler 2003, 8), and punishment is necessary to reinforce society's values because moral bonds foster social cohesion (Cladis 1999, 19), deviance is a representation of unequal power in a society. By applying rules and sanctions to an 'offender,' *otherness* is created by those who hold the power to control the normative order (Adler 2003, 4). In the same way, the abnormal body is decidedly deviant by those in power.[31]

Conclusion

In my research and material practice, I draw attention to the techniques and devices that feminist theorists have employed to undermine the Cartesian modern subject that has contributed to the oppression of others. By using found materials and gendered objects that illustrate hybrid and metamorphic aspects of the grotesque, I playfully subvert stereotypical constructs of femininity. These models of transgression and images of unruly women hold utopian possibilities and the potential for new models of representation (Russo 1994, 61). This new, embodied postmodern subject embraces identity that is unstable, open, changing, and blurs the lines between self and other. Comparing historical methods of discipline and punishment, my work draws parallels to contemporary conditions of social constraint and civic silencing. I question the ways we are blinded to medical and psychoanalytical discursive models that continue to pathologize 'normal' bodies and behaviours. Discourses of the body are crucial to create awareness of power discrepancies and the impingements of individual and collective freedoms, issues that will continue to be the subject of critical investigation throughout my art practice.

The Hijab and the Hoodie: Dress as Politics and Politicized Dress

Boké Saisi

The Hijab and the Hoodie:
Dress as Politics and Politicized Dress

Boké Saisi

On a rainy evening in March of 2012, 17-year-old Trayvon Martin, with a pack of Skittles and an iced tea in hand, was shot dead by a neighbourhood watchman, George Zimmerman, as he walked home from a convenience store in a gated community in Southern Florida. Martin, an African-American boy, was wearing a dark-hooded sweatshirt at the time of his death: an article of clothing that many argue led the watchman to perceive him as a threat. Intensive media coverage of the incident ensued. In the aftermath of the shooting, the 'hoodie' — an otherwise seemingly mundane sporting good — was used to protest the death of Martin; his death was largely viewed as a cogent example of racial tension in the United States in general and of racial profiling in particular. In the following months, numerous regular people and public figures donned hoodies in solidarity with Martin and his family. For Martin, wearing a hoodie on that fateful night was most likely a matter of warmth and convenience. For those protesting his death, it was a clear political choice, inscribing the material with meanings of protest and solidarity. In so doing, the hoodie and its negatively perceived associations with concealment and criminality, particularly when on a black male body, became material for contentious public debate.

A similar fear of facial concealment is evident in depictions of and legislation about Muslim women and veiling, a discourse that is disseminated through mainstream Western media. The hijab — a veil that covers a Muslim woman's hair and neck area — has been hotly contested in the West. While many Muslim women wear the covering as a symbol of religious affiliation and in opposition to Western standards of beauty,[32] the hijab and other forms of veiling such as the Burqa — a full body dress only revealing a woman's eyes — have been inscribed with what many Muslim feminist scholars argue as Orientalist meanings: veiling as a symbol of Muslim misogyny and an impending Islamic threat (Ali 2005; Byng 2010; Clark 2007; Haddad 2007; Zine 2006). In this paper, I will compare the image and materiality of the hoodie and the hijab while employing Roland Barthes' semiotic analysis of clothing and mythology to argue that in the aftermath of the Trayvon Martin shooting, the hoodie, like the hijab, was used as a symbol of political contestation by its wearers, thus resisting views of the material object as a marker of fear and criminality.

The Hoodie as a Threat

When FOX News anchor Geraldo Rivera stated on air "I think the hoodie is as much responsible for Trayvon Martin's death as George Zimmerman was" (Bruemmer 2012) an uproar about the implications of this statement — placing the onus on a young racialized male to fend off unwarranted suspicion rather than inciting law enforcement officials to conduct responsible and lawful investigations — quickly followed. Linton Weeks of National Public Radio (NPR) stated: "The hoodie [has become] a way of expressing support for the Martin family and for the sons of African-American families who bear the heavy burden of other people's negative assumptions" (Sullivan 2012). This comment highlighted how the material item was being used as a symbol of protest and solidarity (**Fig. 1**). The statement countered Rivera's sentiment, who exclaimed: "You cannot rehabilitate the hoodie. Stop wearing it!" For those involved in the demonstrations, they aimed to do just that. In bringing to light the racial implications of the case, the hoodie was used to illustrate how black criminality has been constructed in the public imagination.

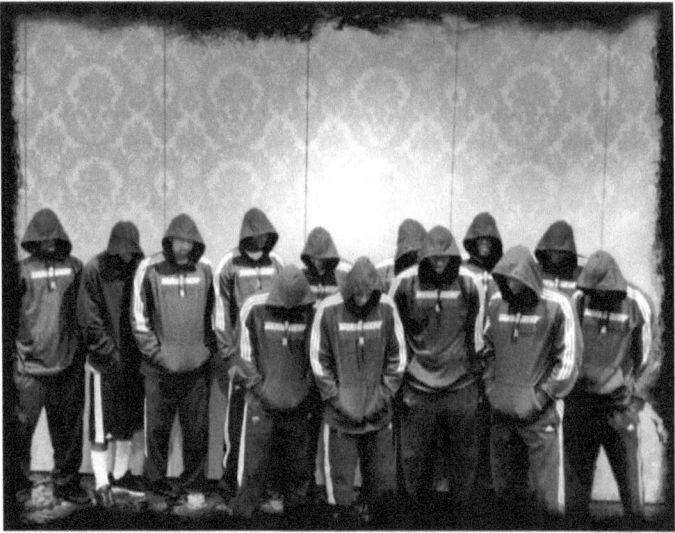

Figure 1. The Miami Heat basketball team wearing hoodies. Tweeted by team member Lebron James (@KingJames) on March 23, 2012. Courtesy of the Huffington Post.
http://www.huffingtonpost.com/2012/03/25/tracy-martin-trayvon-martin-dad-miami-heat_n_1378834.html.

The Champion clothing company first invented the 'hoodie' —a nickname for a hooded sweatshirt — in the 1930s, intended for labourers working during cold New York winters (Champion 2006). The sweatshirt then became a staple of athletic wear best characterized in the *Rocky* films in which protagonist Rocky Balboa dons a hoodie while running up the steps of the Philadelphia Museum of Art (Wilson 2006). By the 1990s, hoodies were a staple in both urban and upscale fashion alike. Designers catering to an urban clientele such as Tommy Hilfiger and Ralph Lauren, as well as high-end design houses such as Gucci and Versace were manufacturing them (Ibid). However, hoodies further popularized as urban, hip-hop inspired fashion arguably rendered the material suspect. Fashion scholar Marcia Morgado argues that hip-hop attire, which is often associated with gangster rap, connotes a "threatening mode of self-presentation, colloquially described as 'in your face'" (Morgado 2007, 132). While the often loose-fitting clothing style is characteristic of skateboard style, surf culture, and prison culture, the association between hip-hop culture and clothing, including hoodies, references gangs and racist stereotypes (Ibid, 134). The material item, which is worn by "college students and soccer moms" (Boyle 2012) is not inherently threatening by any means, but is perceived as such when it is associated with hip hop culture and particularly so when on a black male body. Black criminality is thus mythically inscribed in the material. Morgado posits that controversy about dress is really about "meaning represented by dress: what they are, what they imply, and who gets to decide" (Morgando 2007, 132). In this way, the hoodie's negative association with criminality is dependent upon the cultural and historical context in which it is read and those who get to render the material, and the body it is worn on, as suspicious.

Blackness as a Threat

The hoodie, when on a black body, has been constructed as a symbol of innate black criminality. Kelly Welch argues that the image of the criminally-inclined black male can be traced back to the slave trade (Welch 2007, 276) and is largely perpetuated by both news and entertainment media (Ibid, 281). Racial profiling, exemplified by the Trayvon Martin case, I contend, is a symptom of this pervasive myth.

Welch purports that there is a disproportionate amount of media coverage surrounding black males and crime in the United States. This media coverage particularly highlights crimes such as drug possession. Black males are not necessarily more likely to commit drug possession, but they are more likely to be arrested and imprisoned for this crime.[33] For instance, while 13 per cent of drug users in the United States are black, compared to 75 per cent who identify as white, 75 per cent of drug crime related prisoners are black (Welch 2007, 279). As a further example, the 'war on drugs' waged by the Reagan administration in the 1980s disproportionately incriminated black persons and other racialized minorities, namely for the trafficking and possession of crack cocaine, while white users of the more expensive powdered cocaine were largely unaffected (Gray 1995, James 2005, Welch 2007). As such, African-Americans are contemporarily perceived to commit more crimes based on a higher likelihood for a black individual to be prosecuted for a crime. This misrepresentation serves to inaccurately criminalize the black body.

There is also an incorrect impression that black persons in the United States commit more violent crimes than other racial groups. This is not the case; overall there are more crimes perpetuated by white Americans than black Americans, but it is well noted that black Americans are overrepresented percentage-wise in prisons (Reed 1997, 27). However, mediated images of such crimes, alongside those of black public figures implicated in criminal activity, abound (Gray 1995, 14; Welch 2007, 284). Welch maintains that these images are "so widespread that it would not be surprising if much of American society has subconsciously come to accept the visual portrayals of Blacks as criminals in contemporary society"

(Welch 2007, 281). Black criminality has thus been naturalized and thereby understood as factual. In other words, black criminality is a mythicized notion that is seen in the practice of racial profiling: a practice conducted by law enforcement officials who routinely target racialized minorities during investigations as to increase the chances of finding the perpetrator who, according to this circular logic, will most likely be of a minority race (Ibid, 277). Furthermore, Roland Barthes contends, "myth is read as a factual system, whereas it is but a semiological system" (Barthes 1970, 130). In other words, racial profiling is the process of race being outwardly perceived as an inherent criminal quality rather than the profiling act being seen as the fallacious signifying practice that it is. As such, racial profiling relies on the 'fact' of racialized criminality. Trayvon Martin's death was one such example of this. The hoodie, which Rivera and others accredited to Martin's death, added to the myth of the young black criminal male. Likewise, the hijab has been constructed as a symbol of threatening otherness.

The Hijab as a Marker of Fear

Much like the hoodie, the hijab has been constructed as a symbol of fear and criminality. The hijab, alongside other modes of veiling, has come to symbolize a discourse about Muslims that perpetuates Islamophobia, particularly after the attacks on September 11th 2001.[34] Yvonne Haddad maintains that in "an America traumatized by 9/11, many Americans began to identify the *hijab* as the standard of the enemy" (Haddad 2007, 263). Veiling, a practice that pre-dates the Islamic faith, has also been inscribed with Orientalist understandings of brute Muslim male oppression inflicted upon helpless, victimized Muslim women (Ali 2005; Byng 2010; Haddad 2007; Zine 2006). This is exemplified by attempts to ban various forms of veiling in the name of liberation in Western nations. Furthermore, the idea of Islam as backwards, violent, and oppressive is largely disseminated and exacerbated by news media (Haddad 2007).

Coverage of news stories about Islam, especially after 9/11 have framed the religion and its adherents as innately backwards and in opposition to Western values of modernity and liberty. As a case in point, race scholar Michelle Byng conducted a critical discourse analysis of seventy-two news stories in the *New York Times* and the *Washington Post* regarding veiling restrictions in France that banned the practice for public school students and government employees in 2004, and about the political debates about the niqab in Britain in 2006 (Byng 2010). These bans and debates were precipitated by the European Court of Human Rights' 2004 decision to uphold Turkey's ban on hijabs in post-secondary institutions, which contradicted the United Nation's Universal Declaration of Human Rights' guarantee of religious freedom (Clark 2007, 35). In coverage of these instances, Byng found themes regarding issues of national identity, the integration of Muslims into Western society, and threats of Islamic terrorism. The author argues that while the articles state that veiling bans may be extreme, they create a discourse about forcible 'unveiling' as a justifiable practice. This sentiment was reiterated by columnist Barbara Kay in her *National Post* article "Burka Bans are about Fear, Not Religion." In this editorial, Kay states: "We must get beyond this idea that this face-cover debate is about religion. It isn't. It's about protecting the fragile social and psychological contract people agree to in an open society" (Kay 2012). In inciting the idea of a free and open society, Kay arguably elucidates the dichotomous — 'us' versus 'them' and 'civilized' versus 'barbaric' — reading of Islamic practices that Jasmin Zine argues are pervasive in the West (Zine 2006). Kay implies that Canadian society, as open and free, does not have room for seemingly oppressive foreign practices. That notion was very much prevalent in numerous examples of veiling bans in Canada and abroad.

In Quebec, there have been numerous veiling bans. One such instance was the 1994 case of Emilie Ouimet, a French Canadian Muslim convert who was expelled from her school for refusing to take off her hijab (Ibid). The school administration justified the expulsion by claiming that the hijab would polarize students, likening it to "neo-nazi insignia" (Zine 2006, 241). Muslim feminist scholar Jasmin Zine argues that this association renders markers of the Islamic faith as criminal and destructive; markers that result in a "gendered Islamophobia" in which the hijab on a woman's body is perceived as threatening (Ibid, 239). A provincial ban in 2007 in Quebec exemplified this as well: young Muslim girls were not allowed to participate in sports in various regions of the province if they did not unveil (Ramachandran 2009). This was in part due to the hijab being viewed as a signifier of oppressed Muslim women (**Fig. 2**). Ramachandran argues that "in the dominant Canadian consciousness, the hijab, a piece of cloth, is the symbol for the abhorrent nature of Islam" and that the hijab threatens Western conceptions of modernity (Ramachandran 2009, 37).

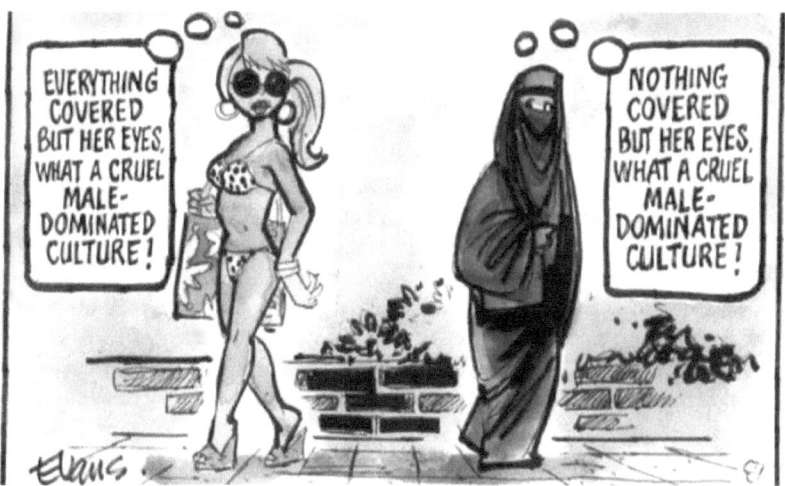

Figure 2. Bikini vs. Burqa. By Malcolm Evans. 2011. Courtesy of Sociological Images. http://thesocietypages.org/socimages/2012/02/22/questioning-definitions-of-freedom/.

The Semiotics of the Hoodie and the Hijab

The perception of both the hoodie and the hijab as markers of fear and criminality depends upon underlying signifying processes that mark them as such.

Employing Roland Barthes' semiotic reading of clothing and fashion, I argue that the hoodie and the placement of the hijab are signifiers when utilizing semiotic theory. In relation to the Trayvon Martin case, a hoodie—which signifies fear—is the signifier, the body and skin colour of the wearer serve as the signified, and resultantly black criminality is the sign. Barthes posits, "the body is in a relation of signification with clothing" (Barthes 1990, 258). In this way, the body works to elucidate the connotations of the material item when on a particular body. Garments within a fashion industry context usually serve a denotative purpose according to Barthes. In other words, "the garment is described according to a nomenclature pure and simple" (Barthes 1990, 236). However, when clothing items are on bodies other than a model, they create an image of an identity that may be perceived differently, and negatively, by varying audiences.

Unlike the hoodie, the material hijab functions as a signified object. The placement of the cloth is the signifier, while connotations of fear and concealment are the sign. For example, a scarf can be considered to be a Western article of clothing, but once it is placed around the head of a woman in order to cover her hair and neck, the scarf becomes recognized as a form of Islamic veiling. The scarf is then, associated with the negative meanings ascribed to veiling. Barthes posits that a "garment can signify because it is worn" (Barthes 1990, 118). This signification, as with the hoodie, is naturalized in a myth-like way, implying that any threat perceived is innate to both the item and bodies on which the items are worn.

Myth can be read utilizing Barthes semiotic theory since myth is a "mode of signification" (Barthes 1970, 107) and a "second order semiological system" (Ibid, 113). When a myth is read, the sign—a final term in a primary semiotic system (i.e. black criminality)—becomes a signifier. This is then read in a larger semiotic relation stemming from a primary system of signification. For instance, if the hijab (sign) signifies a threat in a primary semiotic system, then the secondary semiotic system of myth would be based off of the assumption that the hijab is threatening. This would work to naturalize the initial relation of the hijab, its placement, and a resultant fearful concealment. The re-inscription of the hijab and the hoodie with resistant meanings aims to debunk this mythical naturalization.

Despite these problematic and prevalent interpretations, Barthes outlines the ways in which myths can be demystified. He contends that when you focus on a full (pre-inscribed) signifier, such as the hoodie and the placement of the hijab, and differentiate between the meanings understood from the form (the material item/placement of) the "distortion which the one imposes on the other" undoes the initial signification (Ibid, 127). The relationship between the signifier and the signified is one of rationalization which results in a naturalization of the two. When that inaccurate rationalization is made evident, the myth is deciphered and ready to be debunked. Barthes argues, "myth is depoliticized speech" (Ibid, 142). Both the hijab and hoodie, as material items, have been politicized in order to elucidate the mythicized and naturalized notions of threatening Islam and black criminality, respectively.

The Hoodie as Resistance

In the days succeeding Rivera's comments—about the hoodie being as much responsible for Trayvon Martin's death as his shooter—protests dubbed 'Million Hoodie Marches,' as well as smaller acts of solidarity, occurred across the United States and Canada. The Million Hoodie Marches (**Fig. 3**) took place in New York City, Los Angeles, Philadelphia, and other major US cities. Law students and faculty from McGill University in Montreal as well as those at Harvard, Yale, Georgetown, and more, wore hoodies in order to raise awareness about racial

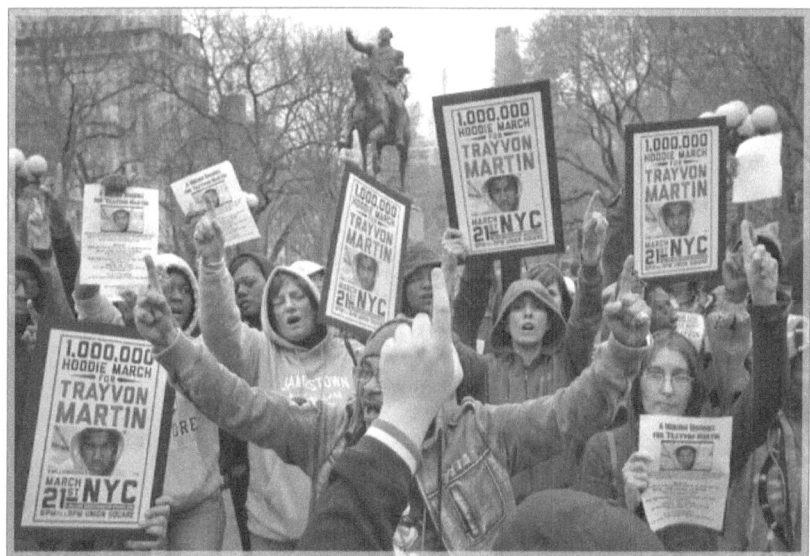

Figure 3. <u>Million Hoodie March in New York City</u>. Getty Images. March 22, 2012. Courtesy of SandraRose.com. http://sandrarose.com/2012/03/hundreds-turn-out-in-nyc-for-million-hoodies-march-to-protest-trayvon-martin-murder/.

profiling (Bruemmer 2012). Members of the California and New York State Senate wore hoodies to assembly sessions, while NBA star Lebron James 'tweeted' a picture of the Miami Heat team wearing the sweatshirts with the hoods up (**Fig. 1**). MSNBC news personalities also wore them on-air. These examples of solidarity illustrate the ways in which the material item was used to protest against the practice of racial profiling: objections that aimed to make visible the prevalence and deadly nature of the practice.

The Hijab as Political Resistance

Similarly to the way protesters wore the hoodie as a form of political resistance, the hijab and other forms of veiling are often used for similar political ends. Muslim women, young Muslim women in particular, have taken to wearing the veil in the United States at what Yvonne Haddad argues to be an accelerated rate after 9/11. The women—mostly second-generation immigrants—who were expected to "shed their parents religious and cultural markings," (Haddad 2007, 253) have adopted the hijab or other veiling practices for various reasons, one of which is to proudly assert their Islamic culture in a time where Muslims are often vilified. Haddad contends that in the United States, this process of 're-Islamization' is also a "public affirmation of trust in the American system that guarantees freedom of religion and speech" (Haddad 2007, 254). Syed Ali makes a similar argument about the adoption of veiling in schools in the United States. In Ali's study, she found that though this veiling occurred prior to 9/11, rhetoric supporting multiculturalism allowed for veiling to be seen as an acceptable practice—despite not always being outwardly favoured—and undertaken to counter negative depictions of Islam in society and the media (Ali 2005). Ali maintains that ethnicities are constructed[35] and in wearing the veil, one undergoes a process of self-ascription, allowing Muslim women to construct their own identity. Wearing the veil is thus a way for Muslim women to wear their politics and highlight how the physical item has been wrongfully associated with fear (**Fig. 4**).

There are multiple meanings when one chooses to wear a hijab or other forms of veiling. Jasmine Zine argues that veiling can be "a means of resisting and subverting dominant Euro-centric norms of femininity and the objectification of the female body, and as a means of protection from the male gaze" (Zine 2006, 243). She offers that meanings of the veil are dependent upon various social,

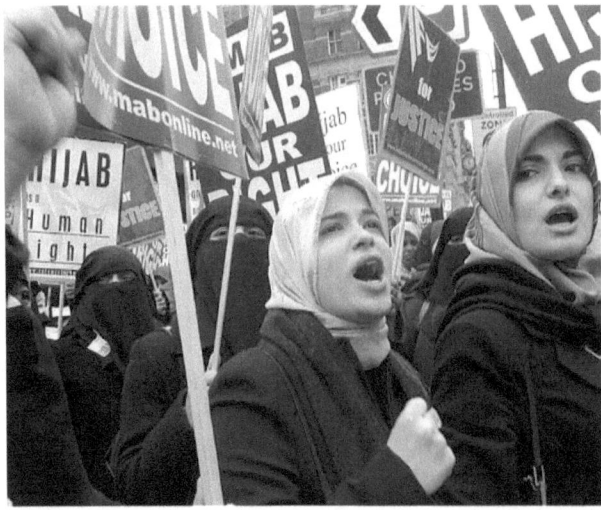

Figure 4. Protest Against Hijab Ban in France. January 17, 2004. Courtesy of flickr user: vptbmuslim. http://www.flickr.com /photos/66854664@N 00/49522548/.

historical, political, or cultural contexts. Fadwa El Guindi reiterates this sentiment, stating that in Egypt "the voluntary wearing of the hijab since the mid-seventies is about liberation from imposed, imported identities, consumerist behaviours, and an increasingly materialist culture" (El Guindi 1999, 71). Thus the hijab is used to protest against westernization while keeping with Islamic values of modesty. However, Ali argues that the hijab's association with extreme religiosity causes the item to be frequently perceived as forcibly worn. Even though, according to Ali, many Muslim scholars argue that veiling is a custom and not "scripturally sanctioned," (Ali 2005, 517) a flawed Orientalist notion remains that the hijab is a sign of male oppression stemming from Islamic culture. That is, Muslim women who choose to veil are not necessarily obligated to do so by either their religion or men around them. This flawed assumption about forcibly worn veils is an example of Barthes' factual system, one that works to rationalize what media outlets have dubbed 'hijabophobia' (Zine 2006, 240). In Ali's study, she argues that young women in the United States, who began wearing the veil, did so despite family objections—objections fearing that the women would be mistreated and viewed by others as oppressed. In this way, wearing the hijab was a way to help 'myth readers' decipher the myth of a threatening Islamic culture by making visual the fallacious signification between this myth and the hijab.

'Symbolic Rebellion' and 'Dress Deviance'

Sociologist Malcolm Brown asserts that while material objects are not innately inscribed with meaning, the system of signification within which an object is contextualized, and the body it is worn on, renders dress politically and culturally loaded (Brown 2001). The hoodie and hijab—as items of resistance—are re-inscribed with political and cultural meanings in order to counter dominant discourses surrounding the materials. These dominant discourses equate concealment on a racialized body with criminality. Brown posits that concealment is perceived as tantamount to an alien identity. In using depoliticized materials that have a mythicized association with racialized criminality, the wearers undergo 'dress deviance,' which aims to use dress as a form of 'symbolic rebellion' (Ibid). In so doing, those who participate in dress deviance strive to attain 'dress freedom' especially within a society with an unequal power structure that regulates dress on othered bodies as evidenced by veiling bans in Western nations. This 'dress freedom' is the social freedom to dress in whichever way one pleases without unpleasant ramifications such as racial profiling. For instance, women who choose to wear the hijab, principally in societies that discourage and fear the material, participate in dress deviance in order to elucidate the multiple meanings that the cloth has for each autonomous woman. In so doing, they bring to focus the ways in which Islamic culture is rationalized as threatening. Likewise, the demonstrations in the aftermath of the Trayvon Martin shooting illustrated how the hoodie was initially associated with an idea of innate black criminality and how, through a form of dress deviance, wearers aimed to debunk myths of naturalized criminality present when one, namely a black male, conceals their face in a hooded sweatshirt.

Conclusion

When blame was placed on 'the hoodie' for 17-year-old Trayvon Martin's death—an incident that can be largely attributed to the normalized practice of racial profiling and the resultant murder of the unarmed teen—uproar soon followed. I argue that the material item was only inscribed with fear and criminality because of the victim's perceived race. Subsequently, many individuals and public figures aimed to use the hoodie as what Brown calls 'symbolic rebellion' in order to highlight the dangerous nature of racial profiling that occurs due to the naturalization of black criminality. Likewise, the hijab is worn, amongst many other reasons, to resist Orientalist views of Islam as threatening, oppressive, and backwards, best illustrated by veiling bans and reactions to those bans around the world. In this paper, I aim to illustrate how meaning-making is created through clothing, and that communication via clothing can be used to perpetuate a myth-like understanding of racialized others as criminally inclined. When this mythicized understanding of racialized criminality is imposed on material items such as the hoodie and the hijab, it works to justify acts and beliefs like racial profiling and Islamophobia. Thus, if material and myth are mutually constitutive, then we may begin to better understand how and why politicized dress is used to protest against negative, pre-inscribed meanings of threatening otherness; meanings that manifest in the infliction of material, economic, and physical violence upon the racialized bodies that don them.

(Re)Activating History: Race, Violence, Materiality, and Interactive Technologies in the Museum

Rachel Fagiano

(Re)Activating History: Race, Violence, Materiality, and Interactive Technologies in the Museum

Rachel Fagiano

The Allen-Littlefield collection, an archive of lynching images, is the most widely exhibited collection regarding a gruesome period of race-relations in American history. Using the display of the collection as a case study, I suggest a way in which interactive technologies can be appropriately employed in reframing the exhibition of violent material through a study of the material nature of images. By carefully examining the controversy surrounding the collection, I explore an alternative mode of exhibiting the lynching images, one that emphasizes their materiality as photographic postcards and focuses on questions regarding the formation of communities of violence and the public nature of racial brutality in the early twentieth century. From this framework, I discuss the role that interactive technologies play in shaping exhibition design, the polemics of using these technologies when discussing lynching images, and the ways in which these technologies can be properly utilized to enforce concepts essential to the particular reframing suggested in this work.

Displaying the Allen-Littlefield Collection

James Allen, a white antiques dealer and self-described 'picker' from Atlanta, spent twenty years collecting 150 photographic postcards of lynchings in the United States — with the help of his partner, John Littlefield. Among the collection they amassed were gruesome scenes: a woman dangling by her neck on one side of the Oklahoma Bridge while her son hangs from the other; a man with his ears cut off suspended from a tree; men and women trussed up on telephone poles. In addition to the images, Allen and Littlefield collected stories, searching for the names of the victims and perpetrators in the photographs. This collection — originally published as a coffee-table style book and later exhibited at the Roth Horowitz Gallery, New-York Historical Society, Andy Warhol Museum, and the Martin Luther King Jr. National Historic Site[36] — has become the preeminent and most widely exhibited collection of lynching images in the United States. As can be readily imagined, the display of the collection in its numerous iterations has been, and continues to be, incredibly controversial.

Defining the Controversy

Spectacle and the Acculturation of Violence

One of the primary controversies arising from the numerous exhibitions of the Allen-Littlefield collection regards the ethics of displaying violent lynching images publicly. When viewing the various exhibitions of the collection, visitors, reviewers, and academics alike were struck by the difficulties in looking at the images. After attending the NYHS exhibition, Brent Staples of the *New York Times* wrote, "I reached my 'limit' quickly and left the room. I returned briefly to take some notes and was on my way, never to return. There is an unbearable measure of horror here that I have no interest in learning to endure" (Staples 2000). In another article, Staples echoed the sentiment of many reviewers, writing, "Mr. Allen had hoped to sensitize us to long-buried horrors of America's racist past. But by choosing to do this through photographs, he chose the most unwieldy method of all. With these horrendous pictures loose in the culture, the ultimate effect could easily be to normalize images that are in fact horrible" (Staples 2000). Grace Hale, in her review of the Martin Luther King Jr. National Historical Site exhibition, noted:

> Viewers are left with an exhibit that is too close to the spectacle created by the lynchers themselves. 'Without Sanctuary's' focus on blacks as victims rather than whites as murderers, torturers or at best spectators—its refusal to ask the hard questions about race and violence in American history — produces an updated version of that old segregating story (Hale 2002, 993).

As demonstrated by the above arguments, many submitted that the exhibitions recreated the atmosphere of spectacle under which the lynching images were originally viewed, numbing individuals to this particular form of violence, and having the potential to reignite old racial tensions.

One of the strongest arguments in opposition to the public display of the Allen-Littlefield collection centers on the idea of 'spectacle' and the nonproductive replay of violence. The making of a photograph has always been part of the ritual of lynching, helping to objectify and dehumanize victims further. Photographs, acting as souvenirs, are often used — according to Dora Apel — to expand "the culturally discursive function of lynching beyond the purview of any particular mob so that both the threat of lynching and its flagrant proclamation of white supremacy could be seen and consumed by an ever more dispersed crowd" (Apel 2007, 17). In this light, displaying the images within an exhibition that would tour numerous galleries across the United States accomplishes the goal of the original perpetrators.

Lynching as spectacle and ritual is firmly rooted in the traditional social performance of public executions (Wood 2009, 24). Indeed, as Michel Foucault notes:

> From the point of view of the law that imposes it, public torture and execution must be spectacular, it must be seen by all almost as its triumph. The very excess of the violence employed is one of the elements of its glory: the fact that the guilty man should moan and cry out under its side effects is not a shameful side-effect, it is the very ceremonial of justice being expressed in all of its force. Hence no doubt those tortures that take place after death (Foucault 1977, 34).

In other words, the performative act of public execution is essential to the execution itself—lynching plays into a long history of enforcing cultural, social and political values through very public violence. Hence, despite differences in intent/message, both the white crowds in the images and the crowds that flock to such exhibitions are drawn by the spectacle of a lynched body (Jackson 2011, 79).

The second main argument against exhibiting the images concerns the 'numbing' effect of a large display of violent images. Many observers[37] have noted that due to the scale of the various exhibitions of the collection, individual lynching images often blur together, re-creating old segregating stereotypes of blacks as victims and whites as perpetrators. The sheer number of images makes it almost impossible to distinguish individual perpetrators and victims but rather creates a narrative in which whiteness in the images is associated with perpetrating crime and blackness associated with being a victim of crime. However, this normalization of violent images can occur on several levels. As Susan Sontag argues in *Regarding the Pain of Others*, 'numbing' transpires not because of the *quantity* of violent images but as a result of viewer passivity. This passivity grows from sympathy, the very emotion the curators of *Without Sanctuary* have sought to evoke. Sontag argues that when viewers feel sympathy, they feel that they are not accomplices to what has caused the suffering, and this in turn leaves the viewer with the assumptions of both innocence and impotence (Sontag 2003, 102-103). According to this logic, the display of violent images, however careful, cannot be utilized for the purposes of bearing witness or productive protest.

Additionally, as Erika Doss argues in *Memorial Mania: Public Feeling in America*, lynching images do not merely record racial terrorism, they habituate Americans to see the death and suffering of African Americans as a disturbing but tolerable site (Doss 2012, 274). Hence, the display of these images has the possibility to be dangerous not only for its numbing effect but also because it makes these violent images tolerable. As the images become more tolerable within popular culture, a certain sympathy towards the violent imagery is fostered—one which, in turn, perpetuates non-action on behalf of viewers.

Protest and Bearing Witness

Proponents of exhibiting the Allen-Littlefield collection see its public display as a chance to reclaim objects of America's racist past for more positive means. To them, these exhibitions present an opportunity for the utilization of American historical memory to provoke conversations about race relations in the past and the present. Proponents contend that *Without Sanctuary* provides a space in which the victims of lynching can be mourned and the perpetrators of the violent crimes named, and subsequently, condemned. As such, the collection's display becomes essential to encouraging a specific way of looking/viewing that reclaims the violent images for positive means.

The concept of bearing witness is central to the discourse put forth by those who support the exhibition of the Allen-Littlefield collection. Indeed, this is the framework under which the Martin Luther King Jr. National Historical Site exhibition of the images was originally conceived. As the curator, Joseph Jordan, noted:

> If we put these photographs back into the trunks, or slide them back into the crumbling envelopes and conceal them in a corner of a drawer, we deny to the victims, once again, the witness they deserve. We deny them the opportunity to demand recognition of their humanity, and for us to bear witness to that humanity. That is exactly what happened in those terrible moments; people who considered themselves decent and devout turned their heads and averted their eyes so they wouldn't have to see. And thousands died because they did so (Apel 1994, 9).

Bearing witness, a concept developed in great detail following the Holocaust, refers to the perpetual attempt to tame traumatic memories through the reconstruction of a relationship between the past and present, to reconcile oneself with that history, and to warn others and obtain reparation (Brink 1994, 7-8). Here, Jordan and others submit that through an exhibition of lynching photographs, a viewer is forced to confront America's racist past and reconcile it with the present, to implicate and redeem those involved in the violent lynchings, and to warn about future incarnations of racism within the United States.[38]

Central to the act of bearing witness is the power of looking. Proponents of exhibiting these images argue that a specific type of viewing is advocated within galleries and museums, which differs widely from the ways in which the images were originally meant to be viewed (Editorial Desk 2000). By a careful framing of the exhibition (via wall text, supplemental materials and objects, and public programming) the viewer is instructed to look at the images only through the lens of bearing witness to the crimes and memorializing the lynching victims within the photographs. By means of this constructed gaze, the act of looking at the images becomes a redemptive one.

In addition to the framing the exhibitions' with a specific curatorial direction the museum, as an accessible space, further facilitates the process of bearing witness. In past exhibition, the galleries and museums were open to the public, with no compulsory admission fee in any of the locations where the collection was shown. The privilege of witness, in this setting, is shifted from the violent, all white mob to an audience comprised of a variety of individuals from a plethora of backgrounds.[39] As lynching scholar Dora Apel notes, "to make common the possession of the look through 'the privilege of witness,' to share it publicly between the blacks and the whites suggests wresting agency from and claiming priority over the 'look' of the mob, of white terror and suppression of black subjectivity that it represents" (Apel 2003, 462). Hence these exhibitions frame the collection in terms that wrest the act of "looking" and agency away from the original, terrorizing and white mob and place it with a diverse audience partaking in the act of witness.

The display of the Allen-Littlefield collection can also be considered a form of appropriative protest and past-present protest. James Allen, the primary collector of the lynching images, notes that in the past a process of 'replaying' violence would begin before a lynching took place through the promotion of the event in newspapers. A photographer, professional or amateur, was central to the occasion, and at times lynchings were postponed until one arrived. Once the lynching was over, the replay of violence began in the form of reproduced images of the event that were sold and collected. Allen, therefore, enters into the present replay of violence by once again bringing the images into public view. However, this is a significantly different kind of replay, one that inserts itself into the anti-lynching tradition (Trodd 2009, 187). While the lynching images were originally produced and displayed by pro-lynching individuals and white supremacists, the anti-lynching movement quickly appropriated the reproductions to display them as evidence of white supremacist savagery. For instance, several lynching postcards were collected and reprinted in the NAACP magazine *Crisis* in 1912 that, not coincidentally, was on display in the NYHS exhibition. As a result, like the anti-lynching protest tradition from which it materialized, the exhibitions of the Allen-Littlefield collection meet lynching within its own historical space—photographic documentation—and hence partake in appropriative protest (Trodd 2009, 188).

In addition to appropriative protest, past-present protest is also a factor that proponents of displaying the Allen-Littlefield collection argue is a positive aspect of exhibiting the lynching images. As Zoe Trodd notes in "Passionate Protest: Lynching Photography and Appropriative Counter-Performances of the Lynching Ritual":

> The images complicated the morality of *looking* and demanded action from the viewers if they were to avoid passive voyeurism. [...] Emphasizing the images' new context as one of reflection not spectacle, education not voyeurism the curators explicitly invited the viewers' participation in an alternative performance. [...] Looking back might move America forward—the whole point of the exhibition [...] was to provoke conversation about history and race relations today, [...] these images make the past present (Trodd 2009, 193-195).

Although none of the curators of *Without Sanctuary* included any explicit calls for action, they did create an atmosphere in which visitors were expected to shift their gaze from spectators to actors through reconciliation with the past. Hence, by forcing the history of lynching into the public memory, the display of the Allen-Littlefield collection can make the past present, protesting a history of silence surrounding America's violent racism.

Understanding the Controversy and Reframing the Collection

While the arguments posed by both sides of this debate are compelling, they employ a false logic that utilizes the discourse of looking as it pertains to photography. What is decidedly different about the Allen-Littlefield collection is that the lynching images are not just photographs but *photographic postcards*. As such they demand a different understanding than simply photographs of violent crimes. As postcards, the lynching images were produced as commodities, prepared with forethought and sometimes commissioned. Postcard photographers not only capitalized on the scene of a crime, but also played a crucial role in producing the crime itself as a 'scene' by turning the images into souvenirs for participants to share with family and friends (Trodd 2009, 193-195).

Focusing on the materiality of these lynching images would initially seem to undercut the argument put forth by the proponents of the exhibition. As photography, the images are understood as indisputable evidence of a specific historical manifestation of racism. However, if the lynching images are viewed as photographic postcards rather than photographs, then the debate surrounding the objectivity of a photograph is brought to the fore by highlighting the reasons behind the production of the image, and in doing so reveals the perspective of the photographer (Edwards 2001, 8-9). If the photograph no longer represents 'indisputable' evidence of America's racist past, it cannot be utilized for protest in the ways described earlier in this work. In addition, understanding the lynching images as photographic postcards could support the arguments posed by those opposing the public display of the violent images. After all, postcards are sent through the mail and can therefore expand the audience and spectacle much further than the boundaries of the original violent crime, the polemics of which have been discussed earlier in this work.

However, I submit that this contradiction is easily subverted upon further examination. Postcards serve as mementos by which individuals mark sentimental bonds with one another. The circulation of such objects maps an imagined community of senders and receivers who share feelings for one another and for the scenes that are depicted on the postcards. As such, the postcards were not only viewed publicly, but also were very much intended for private use. As Shawn Michelle Smith notes, "individuals perform community by sending postcards, and they enlarge community in the same act, for those images symbolically expand a community's claim" (Smith 2004, 122). As private objects sent to specific individuals who shared similar ideological beliefs, the postcards in fact did not expand the replay of violence beyond those white supremacist circles in which they originated.

Indeed, both Dora Apel and Amy Louise Wood argue that when these postcards did enter into the public sphere outside of white supremacist communities, they frequently sparked outrage and fueled anti-lynching movements (Apel 2004) and Wood 2009). As such, an exhibition of these images in cultural institutions that operate as spaces outside of the white supremacist community not only participates in the tradition of anti-lynching protest, but does so within historical structures similar to those that existed at the height of lynching fervor within the United States. These exhibitions can remove the private act of viewing the horrific images from the racist networks to which they 'belonged' and place them within a larger public sphere. Within this space, the images can potentially fuel a renewal of anti-lynching and anti-racism sentiments.

As such, the exhibitions, programming, and public discussions of the collection should focus on the materiality of the images, seeking to frame the lynching images as photographic postcards rather than photographs. In doing so, individuals involved in future displays of these images can guide conversations about the collection away from questions concerning the display of violence to a discussion on the public nature of racial brutality in the early twentieth century and the role that era played in shaping the racial attitudes of today. Specifically, a proper reframing of the collection can lead to a probing inquiry into the nature of "community violence," as depicted in the images. The added advantage to this approach is that it does not simply put forth the opposing argument in the debate concerning the display of the collection. By avoiding the contrarian debate, curators and the institutions hosting the exhibitions can devote more energy towards creating constructive conversations regarding the legacy of violent racism in the United States. By putting forth a unique point of view—one that has yet to be employed in the exhibition of the collection--that reframes the conversation regarding the Allen-Littlefield collections, curators will create an atmosphere in which the merits of the collection become widely evident.

The Polemics of Interactive Technologies and the Reframing of the Allen-Littlefield Collection for Exhibition

The careful reframing of the lynching images would require a new exhibition design by the institutions displaying the Allen-Littlefield collection that, in keeping with the current trends in the museum field, would most likely contain interactive technologies. However, within the specific context of the Allen-Littlefield collection, the use of interactive technology becomes complicated. In order to build a successful exhibition that employs these technologies, it is first imperative to understand the history of their incorporation within the museum and the exact nature of the polemics surrounding the use of interactive technologies in exhibiting lynching images.

Beginning in the 1980s, critiques of the museum field's absolutist stance and protection of Western cultural norms began to emerge (Samis 2008, 3). Coupled with Howard Gardner's newly emerging theory of "multiple intelligences" which undermined the one-size-fits all model of education and instead hypothesized that individuals learn in varied ways (Gardner 2011), these critiques led to a constructivist conception of museum education. The constructivist view has led many within the museum field to understand that visitors, in addition to having a wide range of aptitudes and learning styles, also have varied personal experiences and psychobiographies which shape their experiences within the museum (Samis 2008, 4). In conjunction, these factors have led to a dramatic paradigm shift away from collecting and preserving and towards a greater emphasis on the visitor experience. As Peter Samis argues in "The Exploded Museum:" "The museum of commodifying factor, a temple on high, is dethroned, and the visitor, with whom all experience must succeed or fail, thrive or fall on barren ground, is deemed the final arbiter. The museum is not the sum of the objects it contains but the experiences it triggers" (Samis 2008, 4).

As a result, museums have embraced exhibition design that acknowledges that visitors can experience object information via multiple entry points (Samis 2008, 4). Hence, institutions seek increasingly to bridge the gap between the museum and the visitor through the use of interactive technologies (Vogel 2011). Often these technologies facilitate the ability of visitors to obtain and disseminate information further than they would otherwise, which is particularly evident when examining the museum's virtual presence—its website. Indeed, websites are "undoubtedly the key to the museum's role in the public realm and how the museum manages its relationship with its audiences" (Dunmore 2006, 109). These websites often contain entire digitized collections, providing pre-visit educational materials and downloadable information and images. These materials can potentially reach thousands of individuals who may not be able to visit the physical space of the museum. As such, any images and/or content hosted on these platforms have the potential to reach a much larger audience, numbing a greater portion of the American public to the violence within the lynching images by allowing them to "be loose within the culture" (Staples 2000) or, more simply, once again enter into the visual discourse of American culture. As such, the content on a museum website highlighting the exhibition of the Allen-Littlefield collection needs to be carefully curated.

I recommend that if an institution creates a web-based portal for exhibition content related to the collection, the landing page for the exhibition should include explanatory text that frames the entire show as a display of lynching postcards rather than photographs. This text should make the website visitor aware of the public nature of racial brutality in the early twentieth century and the role that era played in shaping racial attitudes of today. The materiality of the lynching postcards would be emphasized by presenting information about photography studios well known for producing lynching images, documents revealing the staging of lynching images, and evidence of image editing in the Allen-Littlefield collection. The visitor would then be directed to several sub-pages that contain different information including, but not limited to: an interactive map documenting the recorded number of lynchings per state overlaid with a map depicting the current recorded number of hate crimes per state; an archive containing a list—without images—of the lynched individuals, their names hyperlinked to individual sub-pages dedicated to displaying biographic information; a gallery of anti-lynching images culled from the various posters and literature included in many of the original displays of the collection; and an archive of video interviews with the surviving family members of lynching victims.

All of these sub-pages would help to reinforce the individuality of each lynching victim, limiting the amount of numbing repetition of the violent imagery. The website should also contain a section in which recorded visitor reactions would be displayed. The content of the recorded videos would be produced via a laptop located at the end of the exhibition in the physical gallery space. These videos would be carefully culled by the museum curators and educators for display on the website and in the gallery. In addition, no actual lynching postcards would be available for download as stand-alone images; all downloadable material would include biographic information of the individual depicted in the image as well as information on the sender/writer of the postcard, including an image of the text on the back of the lynching postcard. All images on the website should be protected, limiting the ability of a user to individually download lynching images, free of contextualizing information. This would help to limit the creation of spectacle by forcing the viewer to individualize, humanize, and contextualize all of the individuals depicted in the lynching images made available through the website.

As Paul F. Marty warns in "Interactive Technologies," a museum website user may selectively choose to interact with material he/she already has a developed interest in: "It can be argued that personalization technologies that allow individual museum visitors to draw upon their likes and dislikes to create their own personalized set of museum artifacts place artificial restrictions on visitors, limiting the role of serendipitous discovery and their ability to develop new, previously unknown interests" (Marty 2008, 3). This is a particularly salient point to consider when designing a web-based portal for the Allen-Littlefield collection. As a reframing of known material, curators and web-content developers should seek to encourage website visitors to explore as much content as possible. This essential exploration would encourage visitors to learn beyond their set knowledge-bases and engage with topics related to the collection that they may not have had a previous interest in. While the elements of the web-based portal described above provide a good start, they are essentially static web-design elements. This means that visitors can curate their own experiences, pursuing specific aspects of the site that fit into their already defined interests. Hence, another section of the web-based portal should include more dynamic elements in which content is pre-curated and not as mutable—specifically webcasts of curator-led tours as well as streaming and downloadable podcasts. As a set and streaming narrative, these two elements of the website will expose users to a variety of topics that they can further explore through the more static elements described in detail above. Indeed, video elements in exhibitions have sometimes been criticized for eliciting a more passive response from viewers than other interactive technologies for this very reason—the prescribed narrative forces a particular, less-customizable form of viewing (Humphries 2003, 82). This, however, is precisely the type of viewing that is needed to buttress other technologies integrated into the display of lynching images. By taking away some of the personalization of the interactive technology experience, the museum can direct visitors to interact with the content of the exhibition in a new way, one which bolsters the particular reframing outlined here.

Digital technologies, as previously mentioned, encourage visitors to access information in exhibitions through multiple entry points. This has led to a surge in multimedia tours that utilize video, audio, text images, and interactive programs to deliver content to a visitor via a handheld device—often their mobile phone (Filippini-Fantoni and Bowman 2008, 79). Content is made available for these mobile devices via download off of the museum's website or through QR codes in the museum's gallery. However, interactive technologies are just that—interactive. While museums employ these technologies to encourage visitors to enter into a rich and complex dialogue with the content of an institution's exhibitions, interactivity within an exhibition of lynching images has the potential to dangerously recreate the atmosphere of a lynching and exacerbate the aura of spectacle. Specifically, the participatory nature of public lynching has the potential to be recreated by allowing visitors to touch (via the touch-screen technology that is present on so many cell phones today) and interact with a mutilated black body through digital reiterations of the lynching images. Hence, multimedia tours need to take this into account and should be designed in such a way that information is specifically packaged to deliver contextualized information.

Figure 1. Museum QR Code: Example in Four Color-ways. (Barr, July 8, 2012).

I recommend that any future exhibition of the Allen-Littlefield collection should include carefully framed multimedia tours, made available via mobile devices, in conjunction with the aforementioned online platform. These tours would primarily consist of QR codes[40] available on the gallery walls next to objects in the exhibition. These codes (**Fig. 1**)—small images that can be read by a mobile device that is internet- and camera- capable[41]—would direct the visitor to content linked to a specific object.

For instance, by scanning a QR code by a particular image, a visitor may be directed to a video containing interviews with the surviving members of that particular lynching victim's family, biographic information about the lynching victim, a discussion of the community in which the individual lived, the ability to locate the lynching postcard's creation and delivery path on a map that overlays with the interactive map depicting lynchings by state, and specific information which highlights the object as postcard. Like the website, no stand-alone lynching images would be available for download via the QR codes. QR codes are easily updatable (Barr 2012, 34-37) and as such can be programmed to display user reactions to the exhibition content. This would encourage a continued dialogue between visitors, the museum, and educators in which the images can be further contextualized within a predetermined framework.

The use of the aforementioned technologies encourages a very specific type of interactivity. Visitors are not encouraged to interact with or disseminate lynching images separate from contextualizing information. Interactive components such as maps allow visitors to understand where communities of violence existed and continue to exist within the United States. Video provides a space in which the once voiceless families of lynching victims can express themselves openly and publicly. In addition, the capturing and display of visitor reactions via video recording creates a place in which curators can map a new community—one of anti-lynching sentiment rather than the racist networks that existed and made the creation of such horrific images possible.

Conclusion

This work has sought to create a framework in which interactive technologies can be appropriately employed in reframing the Allen-Littlefield collection for exhibition. As the collection continues to be on view in the United States,[42] the exploration of the polemics of the collection and suggestions for future displays becomes particularly important. In doing so, this project fulfills a dual purpose: it offers a way in which the study of materiality can be essential for the understanding of, and interacting with, difficult historical discourses and develops a framework for exhibiting this collection that deals with violent material, thereby filling an existing gap in the literature on interactive technologies, violence, and the museum.

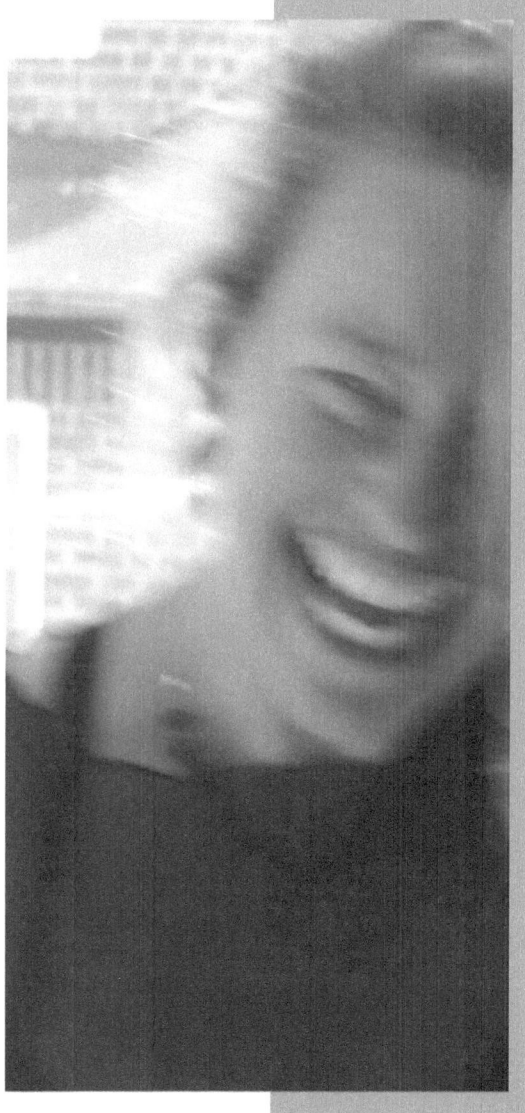

Angela Silver

Archaeologies of Inscription

Angela Silver

Through the discourse of conceptual art, I engage with and reactivate lapsed artifacts of writing technology. The objects I retool and reorder are the outdated paraphernalia of our communication systems, moribund writing tools and their technologies. I examine these obsolescent objects as a method of exploring the gap between our tools of communication, conventional language structure and corporeal experience.

My visual arts practice verges on the archeological. In restructuring the tangible ephemera of our material cultures objects of writing, the work obliquely explores designed obsolescence. From the intimate to the infrastructural, from closets to landfills, we are hemmed in and engulfed by the debris of our outdated tools, the technological 'abandon ware' of our implements of communication. These evocative relics are simultaneously forensic evidence of our relentless impulse to communicate and a notation on technological morbidity.

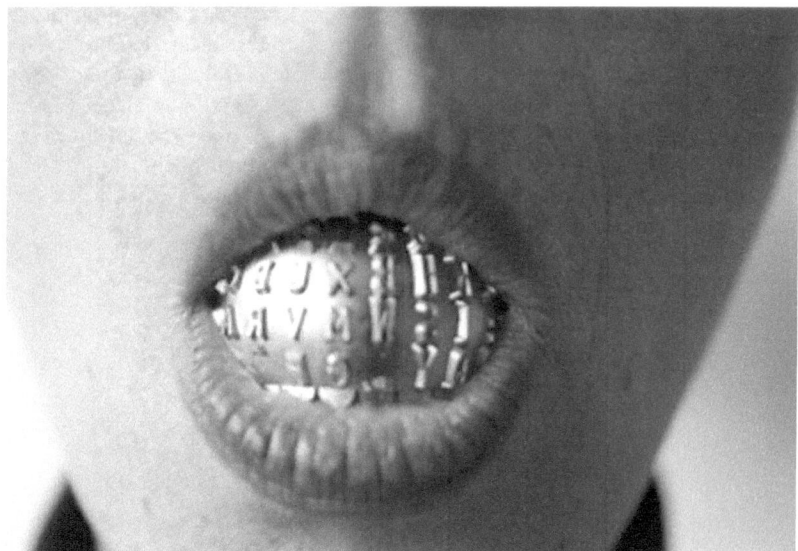

Angela Silver, *Self-portrait*, 2008, 3 ft. x 5 ft, digital Photograph. Collection of the artist.

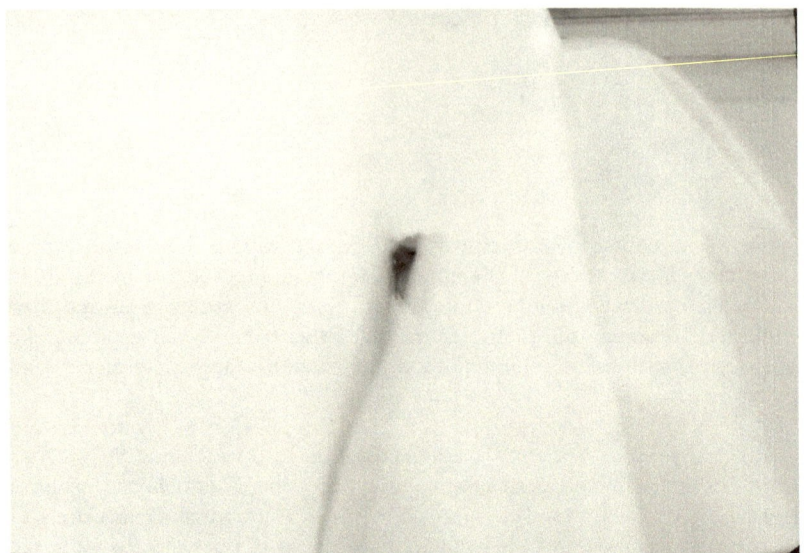

Angela Silver, *Blindwriting,* May 9 2006, Performance, New York. Photograph by Autumn Swisher.

Working with this residue of language, I create drawings, photographs, installations, and performances. These modes of practice examine the itinerant ways in which language inhabits the body. My work looks critically and poetically at Western societies' relationship with our tools of communication, information and its circulation, implicitly revealing the meaning embedded there. One performance, *Blindwriting,* framing the eponymous essay by Hélène Cixous explicates the intersection between written language and the creative act. Blindfolded, I examine the hand and its memory of writing. In the aftermath of the performance, horizontal grey lines trace words in a lattice of penciled text verging on the ruins of illegibility.

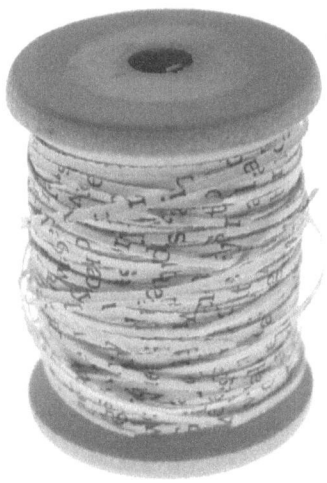

Angela Silver, *Residuum,* 2003-2006,
Collection of the artist.

Much of my work examines and returns to the tension between written and oral representations of language. *Residuum* deconstructs the essence of written language, eviscerating the certainty of text from its structural core. This reconfiguration obliterates legible text beyond the confines of meaning into the visceral suppleness of the alphabet, extracting rigid rules of grammar into a microsite of sounds for our organs of speech to produce. Residuum is a *momento mori* that all languages and their communication systems are structurally pliable processes breathlessly suspended between life and death.

Skimming the surface of the keys, our unique fingerprints push against the ubiquity of the letters of our keyboards. Texting in unison, our thumbs hollow out the core of our languages, extinguishing and curtailing excess letters. *Red Thread Book* concerns itself with a book as a body of transformation. The alteration of its structure is a chronicle of time, thread and labour. Abandoning the book's physical purpose, each line is sewn through, obscuring its text, which disintegrates meaning into fragmentary ruins. In the context of the flow of information circulated and exchanged, sent and received, the book is an archive, an artifact, a wreck run aground.

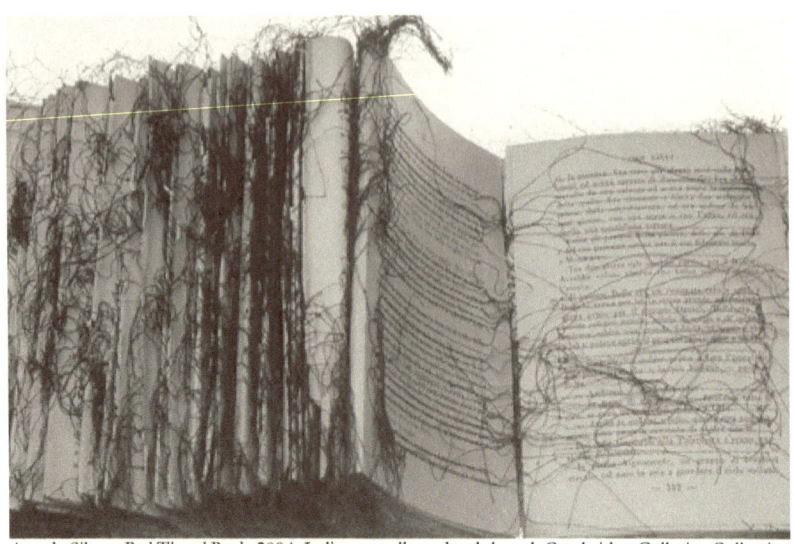

Angela Silver, *Red Thread Book*, 2004, Italian novella and red thread. Cambridge Galleries Collection.

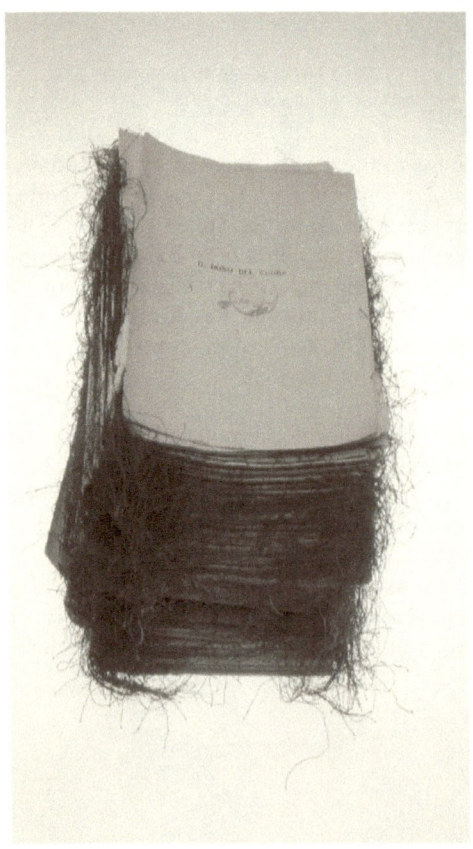

Angela Silver, *Red Thread Book*, 2004, Italian novella and red thread. Cambridge Galleries Collection.

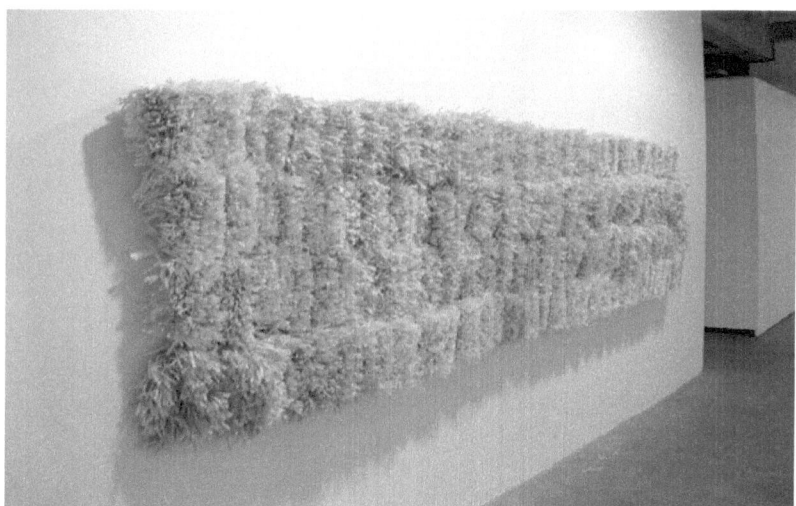

Angela Silver, *Etym, 2006*, sixteen shredded dictionaries. On display at TRUCK Gallery, Calgary. Photograph by Jason De Haan.

From the future of the library to the deep storage of itinerant codes, where will the next repository of knowledge be stored? In the intangibility of transmission, who will have access and ownership, and what will be deemed public or private? My work traces the shadows of these questions as they flow through conduits seamlessly. The materiality of information, from the statecraft's bureaucratic collection and classification to intangible clouds of data storage, my practice shreds, sews, and performs our tools revealing the physical, emotional, and psychological attachment we invest in these devices.

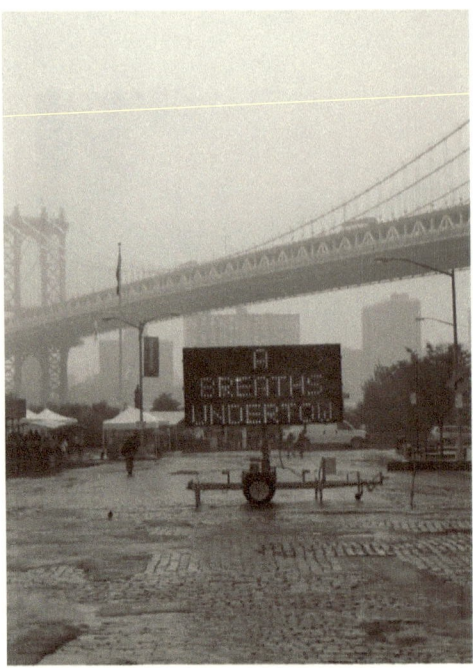

Angela Silver, *Tercet, 2009*. Dumbo
Arts Center, Brooklyn, New York.

I subversively and parasitically insert myself into our lapsed, ubiquitous tools and
filigreed networks. This conceptual and material recuperation is a method to
physically and metaphorically untether us momentarily from our systems in the
plethora of metadata that circulates through us, and the velocity in which we
move through data. My work breaks the back of language in order to reveal its
limitations and weaknesses while simultaneously intensifying and amplifying the
potential poetic space of our devices of communication.

Notes

L'Acadie Fence: A Series of Views
Taien Ng-Chan

[1] See Victor Shinazi's interviews with Parc-X residents in *Two Sides of the Fence*, 2001.
[2] See the ongoing campaigns set up by Montreal citizens demanding a safe passage across the train tracks at the northern edge of Mile End and Outremont. People cut large holes in the fence there so they can easily cross the tracks without going a long way around to the underpasses, and the railway authorities keep patching up the holes, only to have them re-opened: "Passage sur la voie ferrée – Ways to cross the tracks" (Facebook group) https://www.facebook.com/groups/117008484987714, accessed August 1, 2013; and Alanah Heffez, "Citizens mobilize to allow train track crossing" in *Spacing Montreal* (June 14, 2010), http://spacingmontreal.ca/2010/06/14/citizens-mobilize-to-allow-train-track-crossing/, accessed August 1, 2013.

Fired Ground: Warsaw's History in Brick
Samantha Oswald

[3] "Addendum to the Nominations to the World Heritage List", UNESCO, 2008. http://whc.unesco.org/archive/2008/whc08-32com-8BAdde.pdf. Accessed June 28, 2013.
[4] "Polish BBI in €100m Warsaw residential project," *Property Investment Europe News*, 23 April 2012. http://www.pie-mag.com/articles/3059/polish-bbi-in-euro-100m-warsaw-residential-project/. Accessed June 27, 2013.
[5] "Koneser Idea", http://www.koneser.eu/en.html. Accessed March 30, 2013.
[6] "The Warsaw Ghetto", exhibit at The Emanuel Ringelblum Jewish Historical Institute, ul. Tomackie 3/5 Warsaw, Poland, 22 June 2012.
[7] "Old Town and Surroundings", *Warsaw Tour*. https://warsawtour.pl/en/warsaw-for-everyone/old-town-and-surroundings-2946.html?page=0,0. Accessed March 30, 2013.
[8] Employee of the Historical Museum of Warsaw, interview by Samantha Oswald, June 15 2012.
[9] Katarzyna Wagner, interview by Samantha Oswald, Historical Museum of Warsaw, June 15 2012.
[10] "Zota 44 blog", published October 29, 2012, http://en.zlota44blog.pl/?p=2119. Accessed August 8, 2013.

Saint-Henri and the Urban Uncanny
Emma Kreiner

[11] In fact, there are two versions of Hubert Aquin's 1962 film *À Saint Henri le cinq septembre*. The French-language version is 41 minutes long, while the English film is a condensed 27 minutes. The English-language picture is shorter because extended periods of French dialogue have been cut out.
[12] This term is taken from Guy Debord's writings on psychogeography and the potential mapping of journeys in Paris. Debord explained that cities become "after-images" absorbed and internalized through mediums such as film, joining cinema with Situationist cartography. Giuliana Bruno also employs the term, and argued that "The erotics unleashed by the architectonics of lived space escalates in the metropolis, a concentrated site of narrative crossings that bears even deeper ties to cinema's own spatial (e)motion" in Bruno 2001, 67.
[13] Edward Soja elaborates that there is a new missing middle, or 'dumbbell' shape to urban labour markets, that can be attributed to the technological, institutional, and geographical forces intrinsic to the post-fordist economies, and intensified by declining role of unions and the weakening of the welfare state (Soja 2000, 277).

Pornaganda and the Felt Machine

Kaitlynn McQueston

14 According to Stanley Aronowitz, "Commodity production intrudes into all corners of the social world. Its province is no longer restricted to meeting economic needs at a given level of material culture; it penetrates the sphere of cultural needs as well if profit can be gained by this intervention. The institutions of mass culture have in this way become central to the process of reproducing the labor force in proportion to the weaknesses of family, church, and school. Mass culture arises as part of the same development of advanced technologies that released workers from labor" (Aronowitz 1991, 142).

15 For more information on Mid-Century Modern furniture, turn to Cara Greenberg's 1995 text *Mid-Century Modern: Furniture of the 1950's*. To briefly introduce this concept, she offers, "'Form follows function' was a Bauhaus motto, and, in some respects, chairs such as Breuer's *Wassily* and Mies van der Rohe's *Barcelona* functioned very well but if a chair's purpose is to be comfortable, then the commitment to function of modern furniture of the 1920s and 1930s was not always overriding. Elegance usually won out. Their furniture made no apologies for its machine origins. The clean, pure lines of their tubular steel and bent plywood chairs established a new aesthetic, proving that beauty was not the exclusive province of the craftsman" (Greenberg 1995, 16).

16 Joy Parr purports that these few heavily influential scholars were Alan Jarvis, Herbert Read, and Donald Buchanan. Par continues, "The modernism of the National Industrial Design Committee was defined by the influence of three men, Alan Jarvis, Herbert Read, and Donald Buchanan. Jarvis was from Ontario, a Rhodes scholar who studied aesthetics at Oxford and in the 1940s was public relations officer for the British Council of Industrial Design (COID). ... The aesthetics of these three men, and their beliefs about the appropriate relationship between form giving and form making, determined the institutional arrangements and program priorities which defined design modernism to Canadians in the early postwar years. Their modernism emphasized the machine aesthetic, the beauty of neo-Platonic geometric and abstract forms, and the need to educate popular taste to these ideals" (Parr 1999, 134).

17 Parr's articulation of societal interactions with this type of design is worth quoting at length: "Designers at mid-century saw beauty and usefulness in forms governed by mathematics, and found fittedness, with its echoes of survival and biological succession, in shapes which mirrored the mechanical. These elements were articulated as design principles. There were rules for selecting out certain shapes as good design. Even for everyday goods, there were authorities to consult. The look was identified with modernity in the postwar years, a promise and claim as plausible then as it seems implausible to many now. Most contemporary citizens, if bemused by the need to have rules for homely choices, deferred judgment and went about daily doing what needed to be done. And well might householders be perplexed. Modernist design, in theory, could come from anywhere and go anywhere. Conventionally, however, whether made by craft or industry, and found in shops, factories, or homes, modernism was identified with industry, rather than the crafts. Its promise was the promise of mass production. Good design was articulated as a single, universal standard, equally applicable to goods made for industry, and those made by industry for the home" (Ibid, 132).

18 Cara Greenberg further explains the widespread North American cultural interest in Mid-Century Modern aesthetics. "The early 1950s was not the first time modern furniture had been offered to the American public, but it was the first time they lined up around the block to buy it. Buy they did, with the hard cash of postwar prosperity, driven by a sudden voracious hunger for curves that were swoopy, parabolic, ameopoid; lines that were long and low; ornament that was absent; materials that, until recently, had been found only in aircraft factories. Modern had become a buzzword. For a few years, from the late 1940s to the late 1950s, the taste making press honeymooned with the concept. Magazines, newspapers, department stores, even home economics teachers were all in agreement: modern furnishings were the right look for the new age" (Greenberg 1995, 14).

19 Design history scholars William Bird and Harry Reubenstein analyse the role of object propaganda in their 1998 book *Design for Victory: World War II Posters on the American Home Front*. They state, "Addressing every citizen as a combatant in the war of production, wartime posters united the power of art with the power of advertising to sell the idea that the factory and the home were also arenas of war. Poster campaigns aimed not only to increase productivity in factories, but to enlarge people's views of their wartime responsibilities. The poster's viability as a medium of information

and persuasion was tied to its ready access to the workplace and public spaces outside the usual frame of advertising" (Bird and Reubenstein 1998, 1).

The Passport and the Holder
Hannah Jocelyn

[20] These early papers were part letter from an official guarantor acknowledging the origins of the holder, part identification certificate with a list of the holder's physical features, and part justification of the authority of the document.

Gleaning Gendered Objects: Hybrid Bodies and the Radical Potential of the Grotesque
Corinne Thiessen Hepher

[21] *Parlour Window* was an exhibition space in the studio space belonging to Mary-Anne McTrowe and David Hoffos in downtown Lethbridge, Alberta.

[22] A *Red Light* district is an urban area devoted to prostitution, characterized by the red lights and window spaces in which scantily clad women display their bodies to draw men in for sex. In Amsterdam, the red light district dates from the thirteenth century. For more information, look to Abrams 2009.
Freak Show refers to the nineteenth century travelling exhibitions of people with unusual bodies: physical deformities and anomalies, popularized as entertainment in England and America. Deviant and unusual bodies have undergone different perspectives over time. See Fordham 2007, 208.

[23] In *The Metamorphosis* by Franz Kafka, the main character wakes up one morning to discover he is no longer human, but an insect (Kafka 1946, 1).

[24] From 1863 to 1893, Jean Martin Charcot was the professor at the Salpêtrière Asylum in Paris, France. The Hysterical attack was characterized as 'tonic rigidity', 'grands mouvements' also called 'clownsome' because of the acrobatics produced were circus-like, and vivid emotional states such as "terror, hatred, love," and then a delirium of sobbing, tears, and laughter and a "return to the real world." Evidence of the disease was photographed in *Iconographie Photographic de la Salpêtrière* and the patients' 'erotic misbehaviour' was widely publicized. See Justice-Malloy 1995.

[25] While Foucault articulated frameworks that construct ideologies about the necessity to control the female body in terms of correction and cure, he misses a fundamentally important disciplinary method, gender, as an "organized, institutionalized, system of differences that constitutes the individual body and renders it meaningful" (Balsamo, 1996, 21). Feminist theorists have attempted to draw attention to this omission by reminding us that the body is culturally constructed but is also flesh and blood and that both nature and culture are "mutually determining systems of understanding" (Ibid, 23).

[26] Amelia Jones uses the term 'body art' rather than performance art to describe works that emerged in the 1960s to mid 1970s that may not necessarily take place in front of an audience, but involve an enactment of the artist's body (Jones 1998, 13).

[27] Examples of silencing include multiple organizations: governments, religions, social groups, familial groups, and others use fear or consequences to keep people from speaking out and/or use punishment to exercise social control. While a certain degree of social constraints can be seen as necessary for society, governments that employ civic silencing through laws undermine democratic freedoms.

[28] My grandmother, Maria (Buhler) Thiessen (1923 - 2012) recorded by Michael Thys in 2010. In my project, the audio recording was transcribed and given to participants to read aloud.

[29] Figure 09, *Every Body Was Afraid* (2013, work in progress) is a new work building on the project *Ortho Ensemble*.

[30] A 'scold' or 'scolding woman' was one who spoke freely, loudly, quarreled, gossiped or was 'out of line' (Andrews 1970, 1).

[31] A contemporary political issue concerning freedom of expression recently reported by Adam Kingsmith indicates Canadians are experiencing a shift in democratic values. Describing Canada as, "the true north suppressed and disparate," Kingsmith looks at recently implemented legislative strategies: "unregistered civic demonstrations are inhibited and repressed, rebellious Internet

activities are scrutinized and supervised, government scientists are hushed and muzzled, and public information is stalled and mired by bureaucratic firewalls" (Kingsmith 2013).

The Hijab and the Hoodie: Dress as Politics and Politicized Dress
Boké Saisi

[32] The hijab may be worn to reject Western standards of femininity, such as exposing ones skin and maintaining long, styled hair. The covering may also be worn to avert the male gaze. (For a more thorough examination of this topic, see Zine 2006.)

[33] The prison population in the United States is comprised mostly of African Americans and other racialized minorities, and is growing exponentially alongside the number of jails that are now largely owned by private corporations. These corporations use prisoners as cheap labour and the prison system as a means of making profit. Activist and academic Angela Y. Davis terms this phenomenon the 'Prison Industrial Complex' (See Gordon 1999; Gray 1995; James 2005; Welch 2007).

[34] After the terrorist attacks on September 11th 2001 in New York City, perpetrated by 19 individuals who practiced Islam, Islamophobia in the United States was strongly intensified. Islamophobia is a brand of racism targeted at Muslims. The intensification of Islamophobia was evident in mediated depictions of Muslim women and men that portrayed them as a threat to Western societies (Byng 2010; Haddad 2007; Zine 2006).

[35] Ethnic identities can be constructed in varying ways depending on the particular historical period and cultural context in which they are understood. Furthermore, the ways that others perceive an ethnic identity impacts how an individual conceives of herself and thus may move one to rework and reconstruct a particular conception of the self.

(Re)Activating History: Race, Violence, Materiality, and Interactive Technologies in the Museum
Rachel Fagiano

[36] The citation for the respective exhibitions are as follows: Temporary Exhibition, "Witness: Photographs of Lynchings from the Collection of James Allen and John Littlefield." Jan. 13-Feb 12, 2000, Roth Horowitz Gallery, New York, NY; Temporary Exhibition. "Without Sanctuary: Lynching Photography in America." Mar. 14-Oct1, 2000. New-York Historical Society, New York. NY; Temporary exhibition, "Without Sanctuary: Lynching Photography in America." Sept 22, 2001-Jan. 21, 2002, Andy Warhol Museum, Pittsburgh, Penn. James Allen, curator; Temporary Exhibition. "Without Sanctuary: Lynching Photography in America." May 1-Dec. 31, 2002. Martin Luther King Jr. National Historical Site. Atlanta, Georgia. Joseph Jordan, curator.

[37] For examples of various observations, see Williams 2000, Hale 2002, and Jenkins 2000.

[38] While it is beyond the scope of this work, the act of bearing witness has a long and contested history. For an in-depth discussion of the term and a provocative reimagining of what it means to be a witness see Oren Stier Baruch and J. Shawn Landers 2006, 37-49.

[39] Although outside of the scope of this work, this statement does not ignore the lengthy debate in the literature on museums concerning the relative accessibility of these institutional spaces (see: Bourdieu, 1989). Instead, it assumes that access to this collection is expanded to an audience more diverse than the supremacist white audience these images were originally intended for.

[40] Any area in the museum that utilizes this technology should offer free wifi to visitors (Barr 2012). This is essential to ensuring the success of this technology. If wifi is free then devices that do not utilize a mobile data network will be able to access the information available via the QR Code and the user will not have to utilize their data plan costs if their device is wifi capable.

[41] Any individuals who do not have mobile devices that are QR code capable would have the opportunity to obtain an iPod Touch® preloaded with the tour information. Essential to the success of the QR code and iPod Touch® offerings is their visibility/accessibility to the general public. There should be clear signage, as visitors enter into the exhibition, explaining the QR code labeling. In addition, there should be mobile usage guides—as printed pamphlets—available within the galleries for those visitors who are new to the technology (Bernstein, *Brooklyn Museum: QR Code Conundrum*).

[42] The collection is currently included in an installation at the National Museum of African American History and Culture (Bunch III November 9, 2011).

Bibliography

"Andy Warhol Museum: Without Sanctuary Lynching Photography in America." *Arts USA*. http://www.artsusa.org/animatingdemocracy/labs/lab_059.asp. Accessed September 28, 2012.

"Mobile Experiences in the Art Museum." *Futures of Learning*. http://futuresoflearning.org/index.php/Firda_08/tag/museums+in+the+21st+centy. Accessed November 12, 2012.

Abrams, Melanie. "City of (red) Lights." *History Today* 59 (2009): 6-7. http://0-search.ebscohost.com.darius.uleth.ca/login.aspx?direct=true&db=hia&AN=45086602&site=ehost-live&scope=site. Accessed August 1, 2013.

Adler, Peter. *Constructions of Deviance: Social Power, Context and Interaction* edited by Patricia A. Adler and Peter Adler. Belmont, CA : Wadsworth/Thomson Learning, 2003.

Alexandre, Sandy. *The Properties of Violence: Claims to Ownership in Representations of Lynching*. Mississippi: University Press of Mississippi, 2012.

Ali, Syed. "Why here, Why Now? Young Muslim Women Wearing Hijab." *The Muslim World* 95, no. 4 (2005): 515-30.

Allen, James and Hilton Als, Congressman John Lewis, Leon F. Litwack. *Without Sanctuary: Lynching Photography in America*. New Mexico: Twin Palms Publishers, 2000.

Andrews, William. *Old Time Punishments*. London: Tabard Press Ltd, 1970.

Apel, Dora. "Review: On Looking: Lynching Photographs and Legacies of Lynching After 9/11." *American Quarterly* 55, no. 3 (2003): 457-478.

Apel, Dora. *Imagery of Lynching: Black Men, White Women and the Mob*. New Jersey: Rutgers University Press, 2004.

Apel, Dora.*Lynching Photographs: Defining Moments in American Photography*. Berkeley: University of Berkeley Press, 2007.

Aquin, Hubert. *À Saint Henri le cinq septembre* (1962) Dist.: National Film Board of Canada. 27 minutes.

———. *Writing Quebec*, Edmonton: University of Alberta Press, 1988.

Aronowitz, Stanley. *False Promises: The Shaping of American Working Class Consciousness*. Durham, NC: Duke University Press, 1991.

Bakhtin, Mikhail. *Rabelais and His World*. Bloomington, Indiana: University Press, 1984.

Balsamo, Anne. *Technologies of the Gendered Body: Reading Cyborg Women*. Durham and London: Duke University Press, 1996.

Baris, Kilicbay, and Binark Mutlu. "Consumer Culture, Islam and the Politics of Lifestyle: Fashion for Veiling in Contemporary Turkey." *European Journal of Communication* 17, no. 4 (2002): 495-511.

Barr, Dave. "Museums Bring QR Codes Into Play." *MUSE* XXX, no. 4 (2012): 34-47 http://innogenesis.info/2012/07/qr-codes-in-the-museum-context-part-2/. Accessed November 9, 2012.

———. *Kickstarting the Mobile Museum*. March 5, 2012. http://innogenesis.info/2012/03/kickstarting-the-mobile-museum/. Accessed October 23, 2012.

———. *QR Codes in the Museum Context—Part 2*. July 8, 2012. http://innogenesis.info/2012/07/qr-codes-in-the-museum-context-part-2/. Accessed November 9, 2012.

Barthes, Roland. *Mythologies*. New York: Noonday Press, 1970.

———. *The Fashion System*. London: University of California Press, 1990.

Bataille, Georges. *The Accursed Share, Volume I.* Translated by Robert Hurley. Brooklyn: Zone Books, 1989.

Baudrillard, Jean. "The Ecstasy of Communication." In *The Anti-Aesthetic,* edited by Hal Foster, 126-134. Seattle: Bay Press, 1983.

Benjamin, Walter. "On the Process of History." In *Selected Writings: Volume 4, 1938-1940,* Translated by Edmund Jephcott et al. Edited by Howard Eiland and Michael W. Jennings. London: The Belknap Press of Harvard University, 1940.

Benjamin, Walter. *The Work Of Art In The Age Of Its Technological Reproducibility And Other Writings On Media.* Cambridge: Harvard University Press, 2008

Bernstein, Shelly. *Brooklyn Museum: QR Code Conundrum.* http://www.brooklynmuseum.org/community/blogosphere/2011/10/20/qr-code-conundrum/. Accessed November 12, 2012.

Biersteker, Thomas J. "The Rebordering of North America? Implications for Conceptualizing Borders after September 11." In *The Rebordering of North America: Integration and Exclusion in a New Security Context,* edited by Andreas, Peter and Thomas J. Biersteker, 153-165. London: Taylor & Francis Group, 2003.

Bird, William and Harry Reubenstein. *Design for Victory: World War II Posters on the American Home Front.* New York, NY: Princeton Architectural Press, 1988.

Blanchot, Maurice. *The Station Hill Blanchot Reader: Fiction and Literary Essays.* Translated by Lydia Davis et al. Barrytown: Station Hill Press, 1999.

Bois, Yve Alain and Rosalind Krauss. *Informe/Formless: A User's Guide.* New York: Zone Books, 1997.

Borland, Nicole. "(Re)Activating Objects: An Interview with Organizers Cierra Webster and Sam Angove." *London Fuse,* February 3, 2013. http://londonfuse.ca/blog/reactivating-objects-interview-organizers-cierra-webster-and-sam-angove. Accessed August 20, 2013.

Bourdieu, Pierre. "Social Space and Symbolic Power," *Sociological Theory* 7, no. 1 (1989): 14-25.

Boyle, Katherine. "The Hoodie Label." *The Washington Post,* March 26 2012. LexisNexis Academic. Accessed December 19, 2012.

Brassard, Pierre. "Les origines de Parc-Extension." *Journal Le Monde.* October 10, 2010.

Breton, André. *Manifestoes of Surrealism.* Translated by Richard Seaver and Helen R. Lane. Ann Arbor: The University oF Michigan Press, 1969.

Brink, T.L ed. *Holocaust Survivors' Mental Health.* NY: The Haworth Press, Inc., 1994.

Brooklyn Museum. "Brooklyn Museum." www.brooklynmuseum.org. Accessed May 5, 2012.

Brown, Malcolm. "Multiple Meanings of the Hijab in Contemporary France." In *Dressed to Impress: Looking the Part,* edited by William Keenan, 105-121. New York: Oxford International Publishers, 2001.

Bruemmer, Ren. " McGill joins hoodie protests sweeping U.S. law campuses over Trayvon Martin death." *The Gazette,* March 30 2012. http://publications.mcgill.ca/droit/files/2012/03/McGill-Law-students-join-hoodie-protest-Mtl-Gazette-March-30-2012.pdf. Accessed December 18, 2012.

Bruno, Giuliana. *Atlas of Emotion: Journeys in Art, Architecture and Film.* New York: Verso, 2002.

———. "Ramble City: Post-Modernism and Blade Runner." *October* 41 (1987): 61-74.

Bunch III, Lonnie G. "The Challenge of Building a National Museum." In response to question posed by Rachel Fagiano. (Presentation at New York University, November 9, 2011).

Byng, Michelle D. "Symbolically Muslim: Media, Hijab, and the West." *Critical Sociology* 36, no. 1 (2010): 109-29.

Canada's Economic Action Plan. "Phasing Out the Penny." 2013. http://actionplan.gc.ca/en/initiative/phasing-out-penny. Accessed July 10, 2013.

Carson, Fiona. "Feminism and the Body." In *The Routledge Companion to Feminism and Postfeminism*, edited by Sarah Gamble, 117-128. London: Routledge, 2001.

Champion Europe S.P.A. 2009. *Company Overview: History*. http://www.champion-eu.com/company_detail/en/58601/History.aspx. Accessed December 28, 2012.

Chesney, Robert M. and Benjamin Wittes. "Protecting U.S. Citizens' Constitutional Rights During the War on Terror." Last modified May 22, 2013. http://www.brookings.edu/research/testimony/2013/05/22-war-on-terror-chesney-wittes. Accessed June 9, 2013.

Ciborowski, Adolf. *Warsaw: A City Destroyed and Rebuilt*. Warsaw: Polonia Publishing House, 1964.

Cladis, Mark S. Ed. *Durkheim and Foucault: Perspectives on Education and Punishment*. Oxford:

Clark, Sevda. "Female subjects of international human rights law: The Hijab Debate and the exotic other Female." *Global Change, Peace & Security* 19, no. 1 (2007): 35-48.

Conley, Tom. *Cartographic Cinema*. London: University of Minnesota Press, 2007.

Connelly, Frances S. "Grotesque." *Encyclopedia of Aesthetics*. *Oxford Art Online*. Oxford University Press. http://0-www.oxfordartonline.com.darius.uleth.ca/subscriber/article/opr/t234/e0244. Accessed August 1, 2013.

Cope, Bejanmin. "Report from Praga: mega-plans, micro-modernisation and precarious urbanism," *The Journal of Architecture* 15:1 (2010): 105-120.

Crowley, David. "People's Warsaw, Popular Warsaw," *Journal of Design History* 10, no. 2 (1997): 203-223.

Davis, Mike. *Planet of the Slums*. London: Verso, 2006.

Davis, Natalie Zemon. "Women on Top: Symbolic Sexual Inversion and Political Disorder in Early Modern Europe." In *The Reversible World: Symbolic Inversion in Art and Society*, edited by Barbara A, Babcock, 147-190. Ithica: Cornell University Press, 1978.

Deutsche, Rosalyn. *Evictions: Art and Spatial Politics*. Cambridge, Mass.; London, England: MIT Press, 1996.

Dewdney, Andrew and Peter Ride. *The New Media Handbook*. New York: Routledge, 2006.

Di Cintio, Marcello. "The Great Wall of Montreal." *Geist*. November 2011. http://www.geist.com/articles/the-great-wall-of-montreal/index.html. Accessed August 1, 2013.

Doss, Erika. *Memorial Mania: Public Feeling in America*. Chicago: University of Chicago Press, 2012.

Druick, Zoë. *Projecting Canada: Government Policy and Documentary Film at the National Film Board*. Montreal: McGill-Queen's University Press, 2007.

Dunmore, Caroline. "Museums and the Web." In *The Responsive Museum: Working with Audiences in the 21st Century*, edited by Caroline Lang, John Reeve, and Vicky Woollard, 95-114. England: Ashgate Publishing Limited, 2006.

Dunn, Katherine. *Geek Love*. New York: Warner Books, 1983.
Durkheim Press, 1999.

Editorial Desk. "Death by Lynching." *The New York Times*. March 16, 2000. Section A; Page 22; Column 1. http://www.nytimes.com/2000/03/16/opinion/death-by-lynching.html. Accessed October 21, 2012.

Edwards, Elizabeth. *Raw Histories: Photographs, Anthropology and Museums*. Oxford: Berg, 2001.

El Guindi, Fadwa. "Veiling Resistance." *Fashion Theory: The Journal of Dress, Body & Culture* 3, no. 1 (1999): 51-80.

Fordham, Brigham A. "Dangerous Bodies: Freak Shows, Expression, and Exploitation." *UCLA Entertainment Law Review* 14 (2007): 207-245.

Foucault, Michel. *Discipline & Punish: The Birth of the Prison*. NY: Second Vintage Books Edition, 1977.

Freud, Sigmund. "The 'Uncanny.'" 1919. http://web.mit.edu/allanmc/www/freud1.pdf. Accessed July 1, 2012.

———. *The Uncanny.* Translated by David McLintock. London: Penguin Books, 2003.

Gardner, Howard. *Frames of Mind: The Theory of Multiple Intelligences.* New York: Basic Books, 2011.

Gasché, Rodolphe. *Georges Bataille: Phenomenology and Phantasmatology.* Translated by Roland Végso. Stanford: Stanford University Press, 2012.

Giaccardi, Elisa. *Heritage and Social Media: Understanding Heritage in a Participatory Culture.* New York: Routledge, 2012.

Gordon, Avery F. "Globalism and the prison industrial complex: An interview with Angela Davis." *Race & Class* 40, no. 2-3 (1999): 145-57.

Gravel, Pierre. *À perte de temps.* Toronto: Anansi; Montreal: Parti pris, 1969.

Gravenor, Kristian. "Town of Mount Royal's apartheid fencing in history." *Coolopolis* (blog). March 22, 2007. http://coolopolis.blogspot.com/2007/03/town-of-mount-royals-apartheid-fencing_22.html. Accessed August 1, 2013.

Gray, Herman. *Watching Race: Television and the Struggle for "Blackness."* Minneapolis: University of Minnesota Press, 1995.

Greenberg, Cara. *Mid-Century Modern: Furniture of the 1950's.* New York, NY: Harmony Books, 1995.

Grosz, Elizabeth. *Volatile Bodies: Toward a Corporeal Feminism*, Bloomington and Indianapolis: Indiana University Press, 1994.

Haddad, Yvonne Y. "The Post-9/11 Hijab as Icon." *Sociology of Religion* 68, no. 3 (2007): 253-267.

Hale, Grace Elizabeth. "Review: [untitled]." *The Journal of American History* 89, no. 3 (2002) 989-994.

Hassan, Robert and Julia Thomas. *The New Media Theory Reader.* England: Open University Press, 2006.

Higgins, Lesley and Marie Christine Leps. "'Passport, Please': Legal, Literary, and Critical Fictions of Identity." *College Literature* 25, no. 1 (1998), 94-138.

Humphries, Steve. "Unseen Stories: Video History in Museums." *Oral History* 31, no. 2 (2003): 75-84

Jackson, Cassandra. *Violence, Visual Culture and the Black Male Body.* New York: Routledge, 2011.

Jackson, John Brinckerhoff. *The Necessity for Ruins, and Other Topics.* Amherst: University of Massachusetts Press, 1980.

James, Joy. *The New Abolitionists: (Neo) Slave Narratives and Contemporary Prison Writings*, Albany: SUNY Press, 2005.

Jenkins, Lee. "Review." *Journal of Religion and Health* 39, no. 2 (2000): 200-203.

Jones, Amelia. *Body Art: Performing the Subject.* Minneapolis: University of Minnesota Press, 1998.

Jurkow, Gillian. *Rediscovering and Recovering the Front Yard: A Study of Garden Yard Meaning and Owner Attitudes.* MA thesis. University of Manitoba, 2000.

Justice-Malloy, Rhona. "Charcot and the Theatre of Hysteria." *Journal of Popular Culture* 28 (1995): 133-138.

Kadar, Marlene, Jeanne Perreault and Lunda Warely. *Photographs, Histories and Meanings.* New York: Palgrave Macmillan, 2009.

Kafka, Franz. *Metamorphosis*, trans. A. L. Lloyd, New York: Vanguard Press, 1946.

Kay, Barbara. "Burka Bans are about Fear, Not Religion." *National Post*, July 25 2012. http://fullcomment.nationalpost.com/2012/07/25/barbara-kay-burka-bans-are-about-fear-not-religion/. Accessed December 19, 2012.

Kingsmith, Adam. "The Slow and Painful Death of Freedom in Canada." *The Huffington Post*, April 29, 2013. http://www.huffingtonpost.ca/adam-kingsmith/canada-freedom-of-press_b_2946418.html. Accessed August 1, 2013.

Klingman, Anna. *Brandscapes: Architecture in the Experience Economy.* Cambridge, Massachusetts: The MIT Press, 2007.

Krauss, Rosalind. "'Informe' without Conclusion." *October* 78 (1996): 89-105. http://www.jstor.org/stable/778907. Accessed July 1, 2012.

Kristeva, Julia. Powers of *Horror: An Essay on Abjection,* Translated by Leon S. Roudiez. New York: Columbia University Press, 1982.

Królikowski, Jeremi. "Building Visions Through the Drawings of Tomasz Turcynowicz," *Arché* 1, no. 22 (2012): 32.

Kuryluk, Ewa. *Salome and Judas in the Cave of Sex: the Grotesque: Origins, Iconography, Techniques.* Evanston, Ill: Northwestern University Press, 1987.

Lang, Caroline, John Reeve, and Vicky Woollard, eds. *The Responsive Museum: Working with Audiences in the 21st Century.* England: Ashgate Publishing Limited, 2006.

Lee, Anthony W. "Introduction." Photography. University of California Press. April 21, 2012. http://www.ucpress.edu/content/chapters/10777.intro.pdf. Accessed November 9, 2012.

Lefebvre, Henri. *The Critique of Everyday Life: Vol. 3.* London: Verso, 1991.

———. *The Production of Space.* Cambridge: Blackwell, 1991 [1974].

Lewis, Robert David. "Industry and Space: The Making of Montreal's Industrial Geography 1850-1918." Montreal: Department of Geography Dissertation, McGill University, 1992.

Lortie, André. *The 60s: Montreal Thinks Big.* Montreal: Canadian Centre for Architecture, 2004.

Los Angeles Museum of the Holocaust. "Interactive Technology & the Exhibits." http://www.lamoth.org/visitor-information/guide-to-the-museum/interactive technology and-the/. Accessed October 10, 2012.

Low, Setha. "How Private Interests Take Over Public Space: Zoning, Taxes, and Incorporation of Gated Communities." In *The Politics of Public Space,* edited by Setha Low and Neil Smith, 81-104. New York: Routledge, 2006.

Lyotard, Jean-François. *The Postmodern Condition: A Report on Knowledge.* Minneapolis: University of Minnesota Press, 1989.

Mackenzie, Scott. "Société Nouvelle: The Challenge for Change in the Alternative Public Sphere." *Canadian Journal of Film Studies/Revue canadienne d'études cinématographiques* 5, no. 2. (1996): 67-83.

Marty, Paul F. and Katherine Burton Jones eds. *Museum Informatics: People, Information and Technology in Museums.* New York: Routledge: 2008.

Mazelis, Fred "Witness': An Important Chapter in U.S History, New York PhotoExhibit on Lynchings in *Roving Insight Magazine.* February 2, 2000. http://www.rovinginsight.org/library/index.php?content=features-witness-an important chapter-in-US-history. Accessed January 13, 2012.

McCann, L. D. "Planning and building the corporate suburb of Mount Royal, 1910–1925." in *Planning Perspectives,* 11 (1996): 259–301.

McNally, David. *Bodies of Meaning: Studies on Language, Labor and Liberation.* Albany: State University of New York Press, 2001.

Meyer, Karl E. "The Curious Life of the Lowly Passport." *World Policy Journal* 26, no. 1 (2009), 71-77.

Michaels, Anne. *The Winter Vault.* Toronto: McLelland and Stewart, 2009.

Morgado, Marcia A. "The Semiotics of Extraordinary Dress: A Structural Analysis and Interpretation of Hip-Hop Style." *Clothing and Textiles Research Journal* 25, no. 2 (2007): 131-55.

Morgan, Kathryn Pauly. "Women and The Knife: Cosmetic Surgery and the Colonization of Women's Bodies" In *The Politics of Women's Bodies: Sexuality, Appearance and Behaviour,* edited by Rose Weitz, 164-183. New York: Oxford University Press, 2003.

Moskowitz, Marina. "Back Yards and Beyond: Landscapes and History." In *History and Material Culture: a Student's Guide to Approaching Alternative Sources*, edited by Karen Harvey, 67-84. London; New York: Routledge, 2009.

Mukhopadhyay, Biswanath et al. "Spectrum of human tails: A Report of Six Cases" *Journal of Indian Association of Pediatric Surgeons* 17 (2012): 23-25.

Muller, Benjamin J. "(Dis)qualified Bodies: Securitization, Citizenship and 'Identity Management'" *Citizenship Studies* 8, no. 3 (2004), 279-294.

Muwwakkil, Saudia. "Atlanta, the City too Busy to Hate—Once Wasn't." *National Park Service.* November 10, 2004. http://www.nps.gov/nero/greatplaces/shaped%20by%20sitesaudia%20muwwakkil.htm. Accessed March 17, 2012.

Neumayer, Eric. "Unequal Access to Foreign Spaces: How States Use Visa Restrictions to Regulate Mobility in a Globalized World." *Transactions of the Institute of British Geographers,* 31, no. 1 (2006), 72-84.

O'Loughlin, Jennifer et al. "The Impact of a Community-Based Heart-Disease Prevention Program in a Low Income, Inner-City Neighbourhood." *American Journal of Public Health.* 89, no. 12 (December 1999): 1891-1926.

Parker, Reginald. "The Right to Go Abroad: To Have and to Hold a Passport." *Virginia Law Review* 40, no. 7 (1954), 853-873.

Parr, Joy. *Domestic Goods: The Material, the Moral, and the Economic in the Postwar Years.* (Toronto, ON: University of Toronto Press, 1999.

Ramachandran, Tanisha. "No Woman Left Covered: Unveiling and the Politics of Liberation in multi/interculturalism." *Canadian Woman Studies* 27, no. 2/3 (2009): 33-38.

Reed, Ismael. "Buck Passing: The Media, Black Men, O.J., and the Million Man March." In *Black Men on Race, Gender, and Sexuality: A Critical Reader*, edited by Devon W. Carbado, 46-53. New York: New York University Press, 1999.

Robertson, Craig. *The Passport in America: The History of a Document.* New York: Oxford University Press, 2010.

Roguska, Jadwiga. "Modernism in the Architecture of State and Municipal Institutions in Warsaw of the 1920's and 1930's." *ACEE Journal* 4 (2009): 31-40.

Roy, Gabrielle. *The Tin Flute.* Translated by Hannah Josephson. Toronto: McClelland and Stewart Limited, 1969.

Russo, Mary. *The Female Grotesque.* New York, London: Routledge, 1994.

Salmon, Lucy Maynard. *History and the Texture of Modern Life: Selected Essays.* Philadelphia: University of Pennsylvania Press, 2001.

Salter, Mark. *Rights of Passage: The Passport in International Relations.* Colorado: Lynne Rienner Publishers, Inc., 2003.

Shabot, Sara Cohen. "The Grotesque Body: Fleshing Out the Subject", in *The Shock of the Other: Situating Alterities,* edited by Silke Horstkotte and Esther Peeren, 57-67. Amsterdam: Rodopi, 2007.

Sherman, Alizia. "How Tech is Changing the Museum Experience." *Mashable.* 2011 http://mashable.com/2011/09/14/high-tech-museums/. Accessed December 11, 2012.

Shildrick, Margrit. *Embodying the Monster: Encounters With the Vulnerable Self.* London, Thousand Oaks, New Delhi: Sage Publications, 2002.

Shinazi, Victor. "Two Sides of the Fench: A Comparative Analysis of Parc-Extension and Town of Mont-Royal." In *Stories from Montreal: Ethnographic Accounts of Life in North America's Francophone Metropolis,* edited by Gauthier, Louise, Tammy Saxton, Chana Cohen. Montreal: Trickster Publications, Concordia University, 2001.

Smith, Hubert. "The University Film Director and Cinema-Verite." *Journal of the University Film Producers Association* 19, no. 2 (1967): 58-62.

Smith, Roberta. "Critic's Notebook; An Ugly Legacy Lives On, Its Glare Unsoftened by Age." *New York Times, Thursday-Late Edition, Final,* Section E. January 13, 2000.

http://www.nytimes.com/2000/01/13/books/critic-s-notebook-an-ugly-legacy-lives-on-its-glare-unsoftened-by-age.html?pagewanted=all&src=pm. Accessed June 10, 2012.

Smith, Shawn Michelle. *Photography on the Color Line: W.E.B. Du bois, Race and Visual Culture.* Duke University Press, 2004.

Snyder, Robert E. "Without Sanctuary: An American Holocaust?" *Southern Quarterly* 39, no 3 (2001): 162-172.

Soja, Edward. *Postmetropolis: Critical Studies of Cities and Regions.* Oxford: Blackwell, 2000.

———. *Thirdspace: Journeys to Los Angeles and Other Real-and-Imagined Places.* Malden: Blackwell, 1996.

Sontag, Susan. *Regarding the Pain of Others.* New York: Picador, 2003

Staples, Brent. "Editorial Observer: The Perils of Growing Comfortable with Evil." *The New York Times.* Section 4; Page 16; Column 1. April 9th, 2000. http://www.nytimes.com/2000/04/09/opinion/editorial-observer-the-perils-of-growing-comfortable-with-evil.html. Accessed November 3, 2012.

Stier, Oren Baruch and J. Shawn Landers. *Religion, Violence, Memory and Place.* Indianapolis: Indiana University Press, 2006.

Sullivan, Margaret. "Suddenly, the Hoodie as a Symbol of Protest for Trayvon Martin." *Buffalo News,* March 24 2012. http://blogs.buffalonews.com/sulliview/2012/03/suddenly-the-hoodie-as-a-symbol-of-protest-for-trayvon-martin.html. Accessed December 18, 2012.

Szafer, T. Przemysław. *Nowa Architektura Polska.* Warsaw: Arkady, 1972.

Tallon, Loic eds. *Digital Technologies and the Museum Experience: Handheld Guides and Other Media.* United Kingdom: Altamira Press, 2008.

Thomas, Mary. "Art Review: 'Without Sanctuary' Digs Deeply into Painful Issues of Humanity." *Post-Gazette,* September 29, 2001. http://www.postgazette.com/ae/20010929thomas0929fnp5.asp. Accessed June 17, 2012.

Thorburn, David and Henry James, eds. *Rethinking Media Change: The Aesthetics of Transition.* Massachusetts: MIT Press, 2004.

Thum, Gregor. *Uprooted: How Breslau Became Wroclaw During the Century of Expulsions.* Princeton: Princeton University Press, 2011.

Tonkiss, Fran. *Space, the City and Social Theory.* Cambridge: Polity Press, 2005.

Torpey, John. *The Invention of the Passport: Surveillance, Citizenship and the State.* Cambridge: Cambridge University Press, 2000.

Travel State. "Passport Statistics." http://travel.state.gov/passport/ppi/stats/stats_890.html. Accessed June 9, 2013.

Tung, Anthony. *Preserving the World's Great Cities: The Destruction and Renewal of the Historic Metropolis.* New York: Three Rivers Press, 2001.

Vogel, Carol. "The Spirit of Sharing: Museums Pursue Engagement via Social Media," *New York Times,* March 17, 2011. http://www.nytimes.com/2011/03/17/arts/design/museums-pursue-engagement with-social-media.html?pagewanted=all. Accessed December 13, 2012.

Wagner-Ott, Anna. "Analysis of Gender Identity Through Doll and Action Figure Politics in Art Education." *Studies in Art Education* 43 (2002): 246-263.

Walsh, Shannon. *À Saint-Henri, le 26 août* (2011). Dist.: National Film Board of Canada & Parabola Films. 85 minutes.

Welch, Kelly. "Black Criminal Stereotypes and Racial Profiling." *Journal of Contemporary Criminal Justice* 23, no. 3 (2007): 276-88.

White. Daryl. "Review [untitled]." *The Public Historian* 25, no. 1 (2003): 123-125.

Williams, Patricia J. "Without Sanctuary." *Nation* 270, no. 6 (Feb. 2000).

Wilson, Denis. "A Look Under the Hoodie: Op-Ed." *New York Times*, December 23 2006. www.nytimes.com/2006/12/23/opinion/23wilson.html. Accessed December 18, 2012.

Winter, Mick. *Scan Me: Everybody's Guide to the Magical World of QR Codes*. California: Westsong Publishing, 2010.

Witcomb, Andrea. *Re-Imaging the Museum: Beyond the Mausoleum*. New York: Routledge, 2003.

Wood, Amy Louise. *Lynching and Spectacle: Witnessing Racial Violence in America 1890-1940*. Chapel Hill: University of North Carolina Press, 2009.

Zine, Jasmin. "Unveiled Sentiments: Gendered Islamophobia and Experiences of Veiling among Muslim Girls in a Canadian Islamic School." *Equity & Excellence in Education* 39, no. 3 (2006): 239-52.

www.ingramcontent.com/pod-product-compliance
Lightning Source LLC
Chambersburg PA
CBHW032016170526
45157CB00002B/730